What people are saying about *Upskill*

If you want to develop yourself, your people and your teams, read Chris Watson's *Upskill*. Reflecting the growing trend towards self-directed learning, this do-it-yourself guide is filled with practical and innovative ideas that will help both you and your teams flourish!

Marshall Goldsmith, *New York Times* number one bestselling author of *Triggers* and *What Got You Here Won't Get You There* and two-time winner of the Thinkers50 Leadership Award

We live in an age of positive disruption which is only set to increase in the years ahead. The winners will be those individuals who are open to new ideas and actively focus on developing their learning agility. *Upskill* offers a huge range of tactical tools and intelligent ideas and approaches for long-term gain, which makes it so useful for anyone committed to developing themselves or others.

Dominic Monkman, Global Strategy and Business Operations Director, GlaxoSmithKline plc

Upskill recognises that people sit at the centre of their own learning. It's refreshing to read a book that provides individuals with such a range of tools and techniques in one place, which can be accessed whenever they are needed. Chris Watson has clearly drawn on his extensive practical experience in the field. Great job.

Kate O'Sullivan, Deputy Chair, British Rowing, Chair, British Rowing National Coaching Committee

Compelling in its clarity, *Upskill* reflects the latest thinking on how to improve performance by building on strengths – helping individuals to learn at their own pace, in their own time. Anyone working in not-for-profit organisations, in the education sector or in other institutions outside of the corporate world will also find great value in this material.

Eleanor Cannon, Chair, Scottish Golf

What a great wealth of ideas. Using a series of simple tools and techniques that are easy to understand and apply, Chris Watson has created a wonderful resource for anyone dealing with organisational issues or who has an interest in personal development. Every single one of the hundreds of options put forward is worth a read.

Jim Tamm, co-author of *Radical Collaboration: Five Essential Skills to Overcome Defensiveness and Build Successful Relationships*

Upskill is an interesting and thought-provoking book which challenges the reader to take stock of where they are and to consider how they can move forward. Each chapter provides a down-to-earth, inclusive and developmental approach, with the use of welcomed humour hooking the reader in. I can see this being a 'go to' book for any professional!

Steve Johnstone, Director of Higher Education, University Centre, North Lindsey College

Chris Watson has created an invaluable resource, bringing together tips and techniques that really work for pretty much every situation you could imagine. It's a rich source of new ideas and inspiration and a timely reminder of things you knew but had forgotten – and even more than that it's a fantastic point of reference for both classic and bang-up-to-date resources in the spheres of productivity and performance. Highly recommended.

Alison Jones, bestselling author of *This Book Means Business* and founder of the Extraordinary Business Book Club

This handy compendium of ideas is packed with a wealth of proven tools to help individuals take greater control of their professional development and build long-term learning agility. *Upskill* encourages constructive conversations about capability in the workplace, anchored around some of the most valuable adaptive skills. The structure of the book is both engaging and inviting, allowing learners to be more flexible in the way they discover, distil and direct each of the practical suggestions for professional growth. No fillers, abstract theories or tedious stories: just full of easy-to-apply tools.

Curt W. Coffman, co-author of *Culture Eats Strategy for Lunch* and *First, Break All the Rules*

With *Upskill* Chris Watson has curated an accessible, practical and memorable toolkit which any established or aspiring leader should delve into as part of their ongoing development journey. Taking an evidence-based approach, each of the twenty-one keys unlocks a door leading to a rich menu of resources, tactics and strategies. A book destined to spend very little time on the shelf.

Mark Gilroy, Managing Director,
TMS Development International Ltd

Upskill offers a highly relevant and very accessible toolkit that enables the reader to engage with a variety of tools and techniques to enhance their personal and professional development at the point of need. The 'Inspiration' sections provide insights and additional resources that directly navigate the reader to a plethora of supporting narratives, and the book's smorgasbord approach is both flexible and focused – ensuring that individuals can easily identify the areas which will have the most positive impact for themselves and their organisations.

Susan Kane, Head of Leadership and Learning and
Development, University of York

Well-structured and easy to navigate, *Upskill* is a veritable toolkit of tried and tested solutions for anyone wanting to develop themselves, their teams and their organisations – whether they need help attacking a specific challenge or just want to browse for practical inspiration.

Richard Mellor, Global Chief Human Resources Officer, R/GA

Business is facing a new wave of complexity. Wrong response: create more processes and systems and add structures, control and committees – this complicatedness chokes productivity and satisfaction at work. Right response: better utilise people's intelligence, leverage their adaptiveness, strengthen their problem solving skills and grow the individual rather than the bureaucracy. *Upskill* provides tools and guidance to help achieve this, and enables readers to better face complexity without getting complicated – the essence of vitality.

Yves Morieux, Managing Director, Boston Consulting Group

It would be a challenge for any individual to not be inspired by the range of practical strategies that are included in *Upskill*. All the suggestions are neatly categorised under the twenty-one adaptive skills, so you can pick and choose where to focus your efforts – moving away from the one-size-fits-all model. Most books aimed at personal development usually only provide a couple of gems. There are 840 in this book!

Steve Oakes, Associate Director of Education, AQR and co-author of *The A Level Mindset* and *The GCSE Mindset*

In our busy work lives there needs to be a guide or a textbook to dip in and out of for inspiration and assistance, and to provide us with that 'light bulb' moment when reflecting on and developing our personal development. *Upskill* does exactly that. Its format and layout offers easy access without getting bogged down with too much jargon and academic distraction.

Glen Woodcock, CIPD Programme Leader, University Centre Grimsby

None of us can claim to be perfectly efficient and effective. These are personal attributes one can only strive to improve, and *Upskill* is a gem for anyone with that aspiration. Readers will gain immense and individual value from *Upskill*'s rich content by learning concepts, techniques and tools that are new to them, and by being reminded of others forgotten.

Michael Taylor, Principal and co-founder of SchellingPoint Management Consultants

An extremely useful guide to developing the techniques that will unleash the performance potential inside us all. *Upskill* provides a springboard for self-development and personal fulfilment, and is an excellent addition to the field of performance psychology.

Dr Keith Earle, Sports Psychologist, Hull City Tigers

Upskill provides a comprehensive account of personal and professional growth areas which everyone should be thinking about in terms of their own development. It is positive, easy to read and is based on in-depth knowledge of the subject – a welcome addition to the literature.

Dr David Duncan, Chief Operating Officer, University of Glasgow

A user-friendly treasure trove of growth opportunities, with amazingly useful and current content. It's ideal as a resource to support any development work to broaden an individual's horizons, and offers a good starting point from which to promote self-learning and encourage people to take responsibility for their own development.

Kim Ellis, Managing Director, Different HR

In a world of information overload, it is a blessing to discover a well-researched book full of practical tools, techniques and inspiration for developing professional skills that are currently in demand from employers. *Upskill* is a real time-saver.

Dr Angela Armstrong, founder of Sustainable High Performance

This highly practical repository of ideas, tools and techniques to assist with personal and professional development is both accessible and relevant. The serious business of learning is peppered with an irreverence which ensures the reader does not take this important subject or themselves too seriously.

Paula Tunbridge, Deputy Director of Human Resources, University of York

Upskill is a great resource for anyone who wants development but is too busy to access it. The book just begs to be dipped into, whether it be while travelling, during lunchtime or at various points during the day. A bit like a freshly liquidised management and leadership development programme, this resource is there whenever you want a quick sip of knowledge and current management thinking. Business leaders and those in the self-employed consultancy market will find the book especially helpful.

Ruth Cornish, FCIPD, founder of Amelore Ltd

Any format that allows you to understand a concept quickly, and shows you how to make best use of it, is going to be useful. This comprehensive book is a cornucopia of tools, models and techniques that will help leaders and managers improve their skills and be more effective. Flick through and have a go.

Rory Underwood, MBE, motivational speaker and former England rugby international and RAF jet pilot

upskill

21 KEYS TO PROFESSIONAL GROWTH

CHRIS WATSON

Crown House Publishing Limited

www.crownhouse.co.uk

First published by

Crown House Publishing Ltd
Crown Buildings, Bancyfelin, Carmarthen, Wales, SA33 5ND, UK
www.crownhouse.co.uk

and

Crown House Publishing Company LLC
PO Box 2223, Williston, VT 05495, USA
www.crownhousepublishing.com

First published 2018.

Keys image iStock.com/smartboy10.

Leaf and cogs icons made by Freepik from www.flaticon.com, paper
plane icon made by Silviu Runceanu from www.flaticon.com, and chain
icon made by Creaticca Creative Agency from www.flaticon.com.

Quotes from Government documents used in this publication have been approved
under an Open Government Licence. Please visit www.nationalarchives.gov.uk/doc/
open-government-licence/.

British Library Cataloguing-in-Publication Data
A catalogue entry for this book is available from the British Library.

Print ISBN 978-178583352-6
Mobi ISBN 978-178583372-4
ePub ISBN 978-178583373-1
ePDF ISBN 978-178583374-8
LCCN 2018954980

Printed and bound in the UK by
TJ International, Padstow, Cornwall

This book is dedicated to Ami, Ben, Finley and Molly
– the gang of four who challenge me to see the world
through a different lens each and every day.

Contents

Acknowledgements

As you would expect, there are plenty of people who have helped bring this book to life, and, somewhat predictably, I am rather grateful to them all.

Firstly, to the professional team at Crown House Publishing who have made good on their promise to be easy to work with and a truly collaborative publishing partner. Special thanks to the uber-talented Emma Tuck for her editorial excellence and to Rosalie Williams for her tireless commitment to the marketing of the book.

I am indebted to all of the businesses that provided feedback on the skills they valued the most within their organisations, which provided the foundation for *Upskill*. Thanks also to Dr Peter Robinson and Dr Rob Miles at the University of Hull for their expertise in organising the outputs from the Adaptive Skills Project.

Gratitude goes out to clients, collaborators, partners and associates of Endor Learn & Develop for helping with the validation and fine-tuning of the material presented in this book. Also to the front-of-house team at Normanby Gateway for their ongoing loyalty and relentless flexibility.

High-fives to all the other coaches, facilitators, trainers and learning practitioners that I have been lucky enough to work alongside over the years, who cultivated my interest in organisational behaviour. To my mentor Rick Rock for his wise counsel and positive suggestions. Additionally, to every line manager I've ever worked for – the good, the bad and the ugly – all of whom have taught me valuable life lessons in how best to deliver results through others.

There is an old Latin saying, *Qui docet discit*, which means 'he who teaches, learns', and for this reason I'd like to send a massive shout-out to all the learners I've had the good fortune to develop, and be developed by, for being the true inspiration behind this book.

Ultimately, I'm no expert on the human condition, just an enthusiastic alchemist who loves to discover proven, provocative and (sometimes) perverse ways to develop capability in the workplace, so I'm forever grateful to all of the remarkable minds featured in this book who have devoted their lives to a better understanding of the world of work. Many of them have kindly shared their time and expertise to explain their approaches and experiences. It is because of them that this book is everything it is.

The only person missing from this near Oscar-acceptance-speech-esque list of people to thank is the one person who has helped me to pull all of these disparate strands together and make the convoluted seem clear. This is the person who makes it all possible – thank you to my very best friend, the most patient woman in England. She knows who she is.

… the strongest principle of growth lies in human choice.

George Eliot

Introduction

This book has been designed for anyone who is committed to developing themselves and their colleagues, but may not have the time, the resources, the budget or the inspiration to know where to start. It provides a compendium of resources for you to pick up and refer to in your own time and at your own pace: 840 practical ideas reflecting the latest thinking on how to extend personal performance. The suggestions have all been grouped around a set of twenty-one adaptive skills associated with successful outcomes at work and beyond. These key skills can be practised and refined throughout a career and are as relevant for new starters in an organisation as they are for experienced managers.

This handbook of development ideas will help you to adapt and adjust to new approaches and work methods. It can be used to support upskilling through the identification of relevant and realistic options for your professional growth. You will discover a host of proven techniques: relevant articles, quotes and resources, carefully selected videos, novel approaches, time saving apps, topical insights and engaging websites. You can action the majority of the hints, tips and techniques without having to access any external support or invest in any additional outlay.

The material can help with personal development, performance reviews, goal setting, career counselling, constructive feedback, coaching and training needs analysis. The content has been used to add value during management development, team building, project planning, remote working, induction programmes and on-boarding, and has also been picked up by institutions wishing to help students gain a clearer understanding of the world of work. The development options contained in the book are most commonly used to encourage open communication around the recognition of potential talent and evolving work requirements.

Focusing on adaptive skills

The term 'adaptive skills' describes a range of transferable abilities and work approaches which enable people to operate effectively within different environments and work situations. These flexible skills have been found to be an accurate predictor of many life outcomes, often providing similar results to those of traditional measures of intelligence.[1] They are not role specific and can be applied across different settings to provide greater operational agility. Adaptive skills can be developed throughout a lifetime and add value by promoting operational versatility and building personal resilience. As a result, they are increasingly recognised by organisations as being one of the critical drivers of success in today's rapidly changing workplace.

A recent survey of 91,000 employers revealed that the most common skills lacking among existing staff were all related adaptive skills, including management skills, influencing others, work prioritisation and teamwork.[2] Across the pond, a study undertaken by the *Wall Street Journal* showed that 92 per cent of senior managers believe that transferable abilities are either as important as, or more important than, technical skills, with 89 per cent stating they had difficulty finding people who were able to demonstrate these attributes.[3]

Twenty-one key skills

Every skill featured in this book has been included following a ten-year independent study into adaptive work practices.[4] Over 8,000 managers from all business sectors including private, public and not-for-profit provided feedback between 2006 and 2016 to confirm which adaptive skills they valued most in their employees. The research was undertaken by Performance Talks Ltd, with support from the Knowledge Transfer Project (co-financed through the European Regional Development Fund).

The project identified a set of key 'transferable currencies'. These are the workplace skills which are believed to add value to an employee across multiple work situations at any stage in their career, regardless of position. The twenty-one simple, straightforward attributes that resonated with employers are:

1. Ability to influence

2. Commercial thinking

3. Commitment to change and adaptation

4. Constructive communication

5. Creativity and innovation

6. Direction and purpose

7. Effective planning and organisation

8. Enthusiasm for customer service

9. Focus on developing others

10. Interpersonal awareness and diplomacy

11. Intuitive thought

12. Motivation to succeed

13. Ownership of self-development

14. People management and leadership potential

15. Positive decisions

16. Professional ethics and social responsibility

17. Resilience and emotional control

18. Results through action

19. Specialist knowledge and ability

20. Teamwork and collaboration

21. Use of information and data

This set of transferable currencies was robustly tested to ensure its applicability in the workplace. While the labels used to describe each of the skills varied from company to company, the scope and coverage of every one was both familiar and relevant within each organisational setting. Feedback demonstrated that these were the skills which had the greatest potential to provide sustainable value for the majority of employees. However, it is worth noting that while all of the twenty-one items were acknowledged as universally applicable, some organisations prioritised certain skills over others, based on their own customs and/or strategic intentions. Interestingly, the study found no evidence that defined work sectors were consistently prizing the same skills at any one time. For example, while a high proportion of not-for-profit organisations might be expected to emphasise the development of 'professional ethics and social responsibility', there were also large numbers of respondents from this same sector who favoured 'commercial thinking' – demonstrating the fluidity of organisational culture.

The outputs of the study have provided the framework for this book and reinforce the findings of other research into this area, such as recent projects by the University of Kent (which included surveys by Microsoft, Target Jobs, the BBC, Prospects, NACE and the Association of Graduate Recruiters) and other organisations.[5] For example, an analysis of 2.3 million LinkedIn profiles demonstrated that 58 per cent of employees who listed 'communication skills' on the site during 2014–2015 were hired, making this adaptive skill one of the most transferable across all sectors of the job market.[6] 'Communication skills' were closely followed by 'organisational skills', 'teamwork', 'interpersonal skills', 'creativity' and 'adaptability'.

Additionally, there is evidence to suggest that consciously upskilling around these more flexible themes may help with future-proofing careers. A report by the World Economic Forum has identified ten skills which it believes will be in the highest demand by all employers as we move into the 2020s.[7] Their list contains many of the items used to develop the *Upskill* framework, including judgement and decision making, service orientation, emotional intelligence, people management, coordinating with others, creativity, problem solving, critical thinking, cognitive flexibility and negotiation skills. The global report represents the views of fifteen major developed and emerging economies and concludes by saying:

> *Overall, social skills – such as persuasion, emotional intelligence and teaching others – will be in higher demand across industries than narrow technical skills, such as programming or equipment operation and control. In essence, technical skills will need to be supplemented with strong social and collaboration skills.*[8]

Reliable content

While there is growing consensus around the actual skills needed to support operational agility, there is also an increasing frustration among management groups with regard to the way that any upskilling is currently taking place. According to the Chartered Management Institute, over 70 per cent of UK managers would like to provide their staff with easy-to-access, easy-to-consume and easy-to-implement development opportunities which can be integrated into everyday work experiences.[9] However, for this to happen, managers need to know how to access reliable and proven content.

For this reason, thousands of potential options to develop capability were initially considered for inclusion in this book, before being whittled down to a more manageable number. Business owners, employees, human resources (HR) professionals, learning and development (L&D) specialists, management consultants, line managers, team leaders, supervisors and representatives from support agencies, including Business Link and Yorkshire Forward, all contributed to this process, providing practical observations and constructive feedback. Academics from the University of Hull were also brought in to assist with the organisation of the data and to make it easier to access. Every development idea was sense-checked and explored in detail before being mapped against the twenty-one key skills. To provide a consistent number of suggestions for each theme, a total of forty ideas per skill have been included. These hints and tips represented the most robust ideas, which were verifiable, reliable, easy to action, topical and/or ones which resonated most with pilot groups. Where possible, referencing to empirical research and further reading has also been included.

Using this book

Each chapter focuses on one of the twenty-one skills. All chapters begin with examples of how the individual skills may be observed in the work environment. This brief introduction is followed by forty practical ideas to develop the performance of people. Although there is no formal hierarchy to the list of suggestions, all the ideas have been grouped into three inter-related clusters for ease of use:

 Ideas for personal development – the first cluster provides ten introductory level hints and tips.

 Ideas for delivering results – the second cluster is a larger section featuring twenty practical ideas, many of which are focused on work requirements.

Ideas for long-term gain – the third cluster includes ten more suggestions. These more advanced ideas may sometimes take longer to introduce but will often result in greater organisational value.

Within each of the three clusters, all of the ideas for professional growth have been grouped together in terms of how they can support you in your role. Some of the suggestions will be *tools* – apps, templates, downloads and inventories – which can be picked up and used/introduced straightaway. Some of the suggestions will be *techniques* – methods, approaches and procedures – for you to try out, investigate and explore. The final set of suggestions will provide you with information about where to look for further *inspiration* – where to go to discover more, including relevant books, videos, articles and research.

Finally, at the end of each chapter there is a list of *related work skills*. This section highlights the adaptive skills which are commonly associated with each other. For example, there are forty proven ideas for developing organisational skills in the chapter entitled Effective Planning and Organisation (Key 7), but by referring to the Results through Action section (Key 18), you will identify a number of additional tips and techniques to support your interest in developing planning and organising skills.

In practice

This book has been designed to act as a portable resource for you to dip into as you search for strategies and solutions to overcome work challenges. Aimed at the curious learner, the content provides a diverse selection of practical ideas to support your development. As such, it is unlikely that all the options presented will be equally applicable in every work situation. As a starting point, talk with others within your organisation about any existing work challenges and then decide whether these are personal, operational or organisational concerns. Next, look to identify three or four actionable ideas from the most appropriate chapter which could support your progress. Where possible, always build on your own recognised strengths.

The 840 suggestions for upskilling can be used to support self-directed learning, as well as encourage you to connect with others through an exploration of the different possibilities to extend performance in role. The content actively promotes flexible learning and is best applied as part of a holistic approach to personal development which celebrates the informal sharing of learning content. One-to-one interaction with managers, peers, coaches, supervisors, career advisors, L&D specialists, HR officers, teammates and/or sponsors plays an integral role in any learning process and *Upskill* actively promotes open discussions about evolving priorities. The development ideas are designed to facilitate dialogue between colleagues to identify the ones which are the most beneficial to the achievement of work goals and professional progression. Every hint and tip can therefore be regarded as a springboard or signpost to stimulate further discussions and assist with the transfer of knowledge.

Unlocking performance

The benefits of upskilling in the workplace are widely recognised. Employees who are well supported with appropriate training and development opportunities are more able to adapt to the challenges of their roles. They are more productive, more engaged, more customer focused and more likely to stay with an organisation. However, with the amount of demands and distractions faced by staff today, there is less time to invest in generic training programmes unless these initiatives specifically address defined problems. While the short, self-directed learning opportunities outlined in this book are not complete solutions for every training need which may arise, they can – in the right context – provide a rich source of complementary development ideas. Personalised learning possibilities which offer a clear line of sight back to existing work requirements.

From an organisational perspective, this approach may offer additional value:

- Provides a range of just-in-time learning solutions, whenever and wherever you need them, to assist with upskilling – acknowledging the important role of personal choice in the learning process.

- Focuses on the development of adaptable skills which can be advanced throughout a career. These flexible skills are as relevant for new inductees as they are for seasoned executives.

- Assists with the prioritisation of informal learning methods. Supports the adoption of the 70:20:10 model of learning in the workplace, where 70 per cent of learning comes through job related experiences, 20 per cent through interactions with others and 10 per cent through formal training methods.

- Delivers a dynamic snapshot of learning possibilities linked to work requirements. Realistic and achievable ideas to extend performance.

- Encourages the adoption of a more personalised, self-directed approach to skills progression by moving away from the one-size-fits-all model. Places emphasis on what people contribute, not what they lack.

- Ensures maximum use of any training budget due to minimal cost implications, with the majority of ideas for progression costing nothing to implement.

- Promotes greater operational agility, increasing an individual's ability to adjust, adapt and be flexible during times of change. Includes proven learning hacks to help people introduce new solutions to existing work challenges.

- Assists with organisational upskilling by breaking down long-term development intentions into smaller, digestible bites which can be delivered on demand using a variety of methods, including video files, podcasts, books, films, quotes and case studies.

- Recognises that learning is often achieved through a chain of events rather than by one single intervention. Self-managed learning offers multiple opportunities to revisit content using different formats and methodologies which will assist with retention.

- Moves the focus from a series of formal learning activities provided by someone else to an ongoing journey of self-guided discovery. Employees become proactive partners in the learning process. Placing the emphasis on future improvement instead of reflecting on what has taken place in the past.

- Builds management capability by extending opportunities to identify realistic and appropriate development options for developing employees. Assists line managers who may be less comfortable identifying suitable learning options for staff by making conversations about performance requirements easier.

- Positions the process of upskilling as an organic, ongoing and collaborative activity. This mirrors the recent trend towards continuous performance management by prompting more conversations about professional growth between employees and their managers.

- Cultivates the development of a common language regardless of work specialism. Simplifies the use of complex terminology when describing talents and abilities. Helps employees to recognise and share their understanding of the adaptive skills linked to greater operational flexibility.

- Provides a platform for constructive discussions with remote teams, virtual workgroups, contract staff, gig economy workers and anyone committed to their own professional growth.

- Supports career management and succession planning activities. With more people expected to undertake a greater number of job roles in their lifetime, developing transferable skills which are likely to be attractive to any employer could increase opportunities for job movement and accelerate entry into new positions.

- Helps young people to make the transition from education to work. The language used by employers to describe performance expectations at work is often unfamiliar to students and may need decoding.

- Reinforces the importance of applied people skills and the human dimension of work by putting people at the centre of their own learning journey.

KEY 1
Ability to Influence

Ability to Influence

People who are highly influential in a work situation excel at enlisting the support of others to achieve their objectives. They are able to convince their colleagues and are persuasive in their approach. Typically, they can sway the views of others without any reliance on coercion or manipulation. They know how and when to accept the opinions, values and needs of those around them. These individuals have a strong personal impact and are likely to make a lasting social impression. They will often make a significant contribution to the outcome of any important debate. Great at fostering a sense of commitment, they are capable of articulating their views coherently and convincingly. Working across boundaries to build social networks, they can create alliances both inside and outside the work environment by actively encouraging win-win solutions.

Ideas for personal development

> One can only influence the strong characters in life, not the weak.
>
> **Margot Asquith**

Tools

- Structure your pitch using the old marketing acronym AIDA – get their Attention, build the Interest, create a Desire and ask for Action.[10] Remember to highlight the benefits of your idea, not just the features.

Manage the manipulation. Acknowledge the range of different influencing methods used by those around you. Recognise some of the subtle techniques that can be applied in the workplace to construct highly persuasive messages. Look into information manipulation theory and discover four reliable ways to question information which is presented, probe for more details and seek corroborating evidence.

Use ESP to increase your persuasive power – apply Empathy combined with Sincerity to be more Persuasive.

Techniques

Be genuinely interested in others and use people's names. This is the simplest and most effective influencing technique in the world.

Use reciprocity. People are more inclined to return a favour through a sense of obligation. Providing favours which have no direct benefit will make people feel especially obliged to reciprocate at a later date.

Show both sides. Introduce both pros and cons to your idea – acknowledge the cons but always emphasise the pros.

Introduce a highly improbable method to increase your ability to influence in the short term. Try buying someone a caffeinated drink. Research shows that people who have just consumed caffeinated drinks are statistically more likely to be swayed by controversial arguments than those who have not.[11]

Inspiration

Word to the wise. Discover the five most influential words in the English language and become instantly more persuasive. Visit rainmaker.fm and listen to the 'How to Use Persuasive Words' podcast with Jerod Morris and Demian Farnworth.[12] Learn the most effective words to use, simple ways to be a better writer, and some novel methods to personalise all of your messages.

+ Provide options – but not too many. Too many choices can often make it difficult for people to reach a decision. When Procter & Gamble reduced the number of versions of Head & Shoulders dandruff shampoo from twenty-six down to fifteen, it resulted in a 10 per cent increase in overall sales. Look up *The Paradox of Choice* by Barry Schwartz for more examples of why less is sometimes more.[13]

+ Because, because, because. Search out Professor Ellen Langer's research on social influence and discover how using the word 'because' will almost always improve the chances of getting your way – even if the reason you provide is not very compelling.[14]

⚙ Ideas for delivering results

The only way in which one human being can properly attempt to influence another is by encouraging him to think for himself, instead of endeavouring to instil ready-made opinions into his head.

Sir Leslie Stephen

Tools

▨ Apply a simple framework – such as R. W. Wallen's 'communication triangle' – to identify whether you are more inclined to be a tough battler, a friendly helper or a logical thinker when attempting to influence others during times of pressure.[15] This is also helpful for exploring any issues when communicating messages between teams.

▨ Convince your colleagues by following the simple RED model: explain the Reason behind your request (build the why), present and interpret the Evidence and then Draw your conclusion.

Techniques

▲ Influence others by being confident, consistent and clear. Explaining your intentions in a straightforward way and with conviction will send out a message that you have everything under control. This helps people to feel safe, making it easier for them to act on your request.

▲ Talk about and build upon areas of common agreement. Use language such as, 'It's rather like …', 'So, we're agreed on …', 'We share …', 'I can see now …' and 'Let's see what we agree on …' Look up Matthew Feinberg and Robb Willer's research on political influence and discover effective ways to identify areas of common ground and leverage the beliefs of others to your advantage.[16]

▲ Keep your ideas deliciously simple – aim to be accurate, brief and clear. Talk like Twitter. Try to explain the main point of your idea in 280 characters or less.

▲ Build a sense of scarcity. Perceived scarcity will often generate demand. Offers which are available for only a limited time encourage uptake.

▲ Be aware of the primacy–recency effect when attempting to persuade others. Information presented at the beginning (primacy) and end (recency) of any communication will often be retained better than information presented in-between.

▲ Don't just listen – acknowledge. People are usually more willing to meet others halfway if they feel they are recognised, understood and appreciated. Be fluid and flexible. Modify your position in light of others' views and suggestions. Use networking techniques to build rapport – ask questions, find connections and move in those directions.

▲ Construct great stories. Infuse some drama into your existing ideas to make sense of complex situations. Present your thoughts in rich pictures and vivid words. Appeal to both visual and auditory thinkers. Adapt the delivery and style of your messages for different audiences. Alter the tone and the language – but always keep the message the same.

▲ Use sticky notes if you want people to respond positively. If you attach a sticky note to your letters, surveys and mailshots, you will yield significantly better results.[17] While this works best when you write 'thank you' and put your signature on the note, research also reveals that simply adding a blank note onto any message is more effective than sending printed materials without one.

▲ Search for opportunities to build connectivity – be a facilitator and put the right people in touch with each other. Request to run more workgroups and project teams and build relationships with internal customers.

▲ Consider whether you have access to multiple sources of information. Can you influence others by sharing this data and expertise? Use facts to build up your case, then humanise it with credible endorsements, testimonials and case studies.

▲ When providing either positive feedback or developmental feedback, always ask the other person's permission first: 'Can I give you some feedback?' It strengthens receptivity before you even start.

▲ Pace yourself. Persuasive presenters instinctively adjust the speed of their delivery based on the response of their audience. When talking to those who are in agreement with their message, they will tend to speak more slowly. If they are presenting to people who are more sceptical about the content, they will speak more quickly. Research has revealed that the delivery of a deliberately faster than normal rate of speech is likely to be more persuasive with audiences who are unconvinced about the message.[18]

Inspiration

✛ Scour second-hand bookshops and get hold of a dusty old copy of *How to Win Friends and Influence People* by Dale Carnegie.[19]

✛ Because you're worth it. Watch Casey Brown's TED Talk 'Know Your Worth and Then Ask for It', and discover ways to overcome self-doubt so you can confidently earn what you deserve.[20]

⊹ Take centre stage. Look up the research findings of Priya Raghubir and Ana Valenzuela to find out why occupying the central position in any group meeting can both enhance your ability to create a favourable impression and also significantly improve your chances of influencing others.[21]

⊹ Get people to commit to just part of your request. If they do so, they will be far more likely to honour all of the request at a later stage. Watch Dr Richard Wiseman's 'Secret Persuasion Mind Trick' on YouTube to see how this works.[22]

⊹ Be more positive – read *Yes! 60 Secrets from the Science of Persuasion* by Noah Goldstein, Steve Martin and Robert Cialdini.[23] Based on scientific research, this handy book reveals how the psychology of persuasion can help you to achieve more of what you want.

⊹ Pick up a copy of *Influencer: The Power to Change Anything* by Kerry Patterson et al.[24]

 # Ideas for long-term gain

> *Example is not the main thing [in influencing others]. It is the only thing.*
>
> **Albert Schweitzer**

Tools

▦ Complete an Insights Discovery profile and receive feedback on your preferred way of influencing others.[25] Find out how an understanding of the colour preferences model will help you to build rapport, adapt your approach and strengthen relationships.

▦ Explore how to progressively increase your influence at work by applying Gene Dalton and Paul Thompson's Four Stages of Contribution model.[26] Discover the behaviours most associated with positive influence across any organisation.

■ Ensure your ideas survive by making them sticky. Apply Chip and Dan Heath's SUCCESs technique.[27]

Techniques

▲ Recognise that your own character is often your greatest source of influence. Are you regarded as authentic and trustworthy? Do you always follow through on commitments? Studies suggest that people will trust you more if you reveal a minor weakness upfront.[28] When highlighting a fault, select a minor one which has two sides to it: 'We certainly aren't the cheapest, but all our services come with a reassuring five-year guarantee.' Similarly, people who take responsibility when something goes wrong are also more trusted than people who blame others or external circumstances.

▲ Be graciously disruptive. Regularly challenge conventional wisdom, but instead of dismissing things for the sake of being disruptive, uses phrases such as 'what if?' and 'why not?' to help you develop a reputation as someone who constantly strives to make things better.

▲ Influence by providing evidence of social proof – people like to do things they see others doing, so use testimonials, endorsements, case studies and media coverage to support your message. Also use social norms and modelling behaviour to reinforce the behaviours you want to see.

▲ Persuade fewer people. Scientists at Rensselaer Polytechnic Institute found that when just 10 per cent of a given population holds an unshakable belief, the belief was likely to be adopted by the majority.[29] Aim to get at least 10 per cent of your workgroup really committed to your idea and the chances are that the idea will spread like a flame.

▲ People will always commit themselves to a world they help to create, so minimise any temptation to coerce others and instead influence by getting them involved. Spend time in conversation with people and build allies to support your cause. Try to accommodate the other person's ideas before adding your own.

Inspiration

+ Reach for the classics. *Getting to Yes: Negotiating an Agreement Without Giving In* by Roger Fisher and William Ury provides a solid grounding in applied negotiation skills.[30] It is full of practical advice on working with others to resolve disputes, all based on real-life application.

+ Uncover the subtle, secret influencers which affect our decision making by taking a peek at *Invisible Influence: The Hidden Forces that Shape Behaviour* by Jonah Berger.[31]

 # Related work skills

Commitment to Change and Adaptation (3), Constructive Communication (4), Direction and Purpose (6), Enthusiasm for Customer Service (8), Interpersonal Awareness and Diplomacy (10), People Management and Leadership Potential (14).

KEY 2

Commercial Thinking

Commercial Thinking

People who prioritise commercial consequences will recognise the financial realities affecting an organisation and use fiscal considerations to make timely decisions. They are likely to excel at linking their work priorities to the bigger picture. Often, they will strive to understand the relationship between different departments within an organisation and acknowledge the contribution that each area makes. These enterprising individuals focus on improving results by managing costs effectively. They can step back from events and consider the wider implications. Great at anticipating future possibilities, they can map out the way ahead by scanning work horizons to identify the most profitable long-term opportunities.

 ## Ideas for personal development

> *Be undeniably good. No marketing effort or social media buzzword can be a substitute for that.*
>
> **Anthony Volodkin**

Tools

- Set a Google Alert for specific themes within your industry or sector to keep abreast of the latest happenings.

- Present a SWOT analysis of the entire organisation to your line manager – highlighting all the relevant Strengths, Weaknesses, Opportunities and Threats.

- Subscribe online to the *Times*, *Financial Times*, *Guardian* or *Telegraph*, then create your own Flipboard with commercial information pages.

Techniques

▲ Know your lingo – make a list of any popular terms, phrases or acronyms. Actively flag up language and terms which are complex or hard to decipher.

▲ Explain the purpose of your organisation to someone who knows nothing about it.

▲ Spend time with your line manager to unpick significant costs and overheads. Know your department's contribution to the bottom line. Then approach whoever runs your finance function and ask to spend some time with them to gain a greater understanding of your wider financial position and any obstacles to success.

▲ Grab a copy of your organisation's most recent profit and loss statement, balance sheet and cash flow. Ask questions about items you are unsure about.

▲ Talk to your customers more often. Build a strong understanding as to why your clients buy from you instead of your competitors. Find out more about how and when they use your products and services.

Inspiration

✦ Pick up a few biographies of entrepreneurs and business leaders you admire. Learn from their personal journeys and life lessons. If you aren't sure where to start, visit biography.com or uk.businessinsider.com. As self-made millionaire T. Harv Eker once said, 'Successful people look at other successful people as a means to motivate themselves.' One of the best starting points is to read about someone who's already done it.

✦ Take a break and gain some perspective by watching *Glengarry Glen Ross* (1992) starring Al Pacino – one of a handful of insightful films about the realities of working life.

⚙ Ideas for delivering results

> *An entrepreneur is someone who has a vision for something and a want to create.*
>
> **David Karp**

Tools

▨ Eliminate distractions but stay up to date with trends in your field by using the Feedly app. It captures and organises articles of interest from around the web, ready for you to read when you have more time.

▨ Inspire everyone to talk about the wider environment by introducing a PESTLE or Cultural Web exercise at your next meeting. Both of these business analysis tools can be used to create useful conversations about the marketplace in which you operate.

▨ Book yourself onto a critical thinking skills course and apply the techniques you have learned to future business problems.

▨ Use Twitter and other social media platforms to follow your competitors and track emerging trends.

▨ Introduce the 3C's model to develop a more strategic view of the factors needed for success.[32] It suggests that competitive advantage can only be achieved by considering the Customer, the Competitors and the Corporation (or organisation). To help others understand your commercial challenges, consider three more C's: what is the Context of the decision to be made? Do you have Clarity in terms of the scope? What are the Criteria used (the commercial factors used to select options)?

Techniques

▲ Develop a reputation for being someone who is passionate about managing people, resources and materials to drive profitability.

▲ Recognise and acknowledge both formal and informal relationships between different departments. Request a meeting with different managers across the business to see how their function is organised and meet key personnel. Use internal networking opportunities to extend your own commercial judgement.

▲ Ring-fence one day to spend with a key customer/end user to identify and agree present and future needs.

▲ Begin to create a personal log to evidence how you and your team have adapted to evolving markets.

▲ Identify where you need to be disruptive and then disrupt. Follow the lead of spiritual guru Deepak Chopra and ask yourself: 'Is what I'm going to do really so cutting edge that nobody else is doing it?'[33]

▲ Attend two sector-specific business groups in the next six months and share your observations with your team.

▲ Become your team's authority on competitor activity – build credibility and value by extending your intimacy with the wider marketplace. Get a copy of your competitors' accounts and annual report. Understand your rivals' products and services.

▲ Develop a simple diagram to illustrate your organisation's supply chain and share it with all new starters at their induction.

▲ Apply a commercial perspective to everyday tasks – include financial impact, margin and overhead considerations within every meeting agenda. Intervene when required to ensure that others' energies are directed towards the most commercially viable pursuits.

▲ Arrange informal training sessions and cross-functional meetings to support the development of your team's commercial skills.

▲ Volunteer to contribute towards the creation of your next strategic plan (even if this only involves overseeing the contributions of others).

▲ Regularly explore alternative ideas and ways of working to gain cost savings. Use knowledge of your marketplace to anticipate changes when budgeting for the future.

Inspiration

✦ Grab a copy of *How to Think Strategically* by Davide Sola and Jerome Couturier and learn to step back from day-to-day issues by maintaining a long-term perspective when dealing with short-term issues. [34]

✦ Subscribe to selected industry newsletters and blogs. Find out who the movers and shakers are. Find out what makes them shake. Think big. Start reading *The Economist*, *The Drum*, *Business Matters*, *Harvard Business Review*, *Forbes*, *Fast Company* and other titles for an up-to-date blend of market predictions and financial insights from around the world.

✦ Take a dip. Find out why strategic quitting sometimes works by reading *The Dip* by Seth Godin.[35] Learn about the dip and why winners sometimes quit and quitters sometimes win.

 # Ideas for long-term gain

> *The purpose of business is to create and keep a customer.*
> **Peter F. Drucker**

Tools

▪ Use the McKinsey 7S Framework to encourage a more holistic approach to organisational change.[36]

Incentivise others to identify new avenues and commercial opportunities to add greater value and drive profitability. Use the entrepreneurial acronym ABA – Always Be Adapting. Be an ambassador for the creation of a more agile, change orientated culture which is receptive to innovation.

Techniques

Introduce yourself to prominent local entrepreneurs and investigate any differences of approach to financial planning methods.

Investigate mosaic theory and find out how using this approach can help you to reach informed conclusions about the financial health of other organisations by piecing together bits of publicly available information.

Work *on* the business, not *in* the business. Cultivate a franchise prototype mindset by focusing on how every single customer or end user will have a rich and consistent experience – wherever they are. Commercially, this requires a well-documented system so that, ultimately, the department or business can operate and thrive on its own.

Provide coaching and guidance to others to increase your personal visibility and help you to influence wider stakeholder expectations. Coaching staff across the organisation will extend your own questioning and consultancy skills and assist with the identification of emerging issues. Working with aspirational people from other departments will encourage you to consistently apply solution orientated language. By promoting an approach which champions the ongoing consideration of cost versus value, you will also remind others of the commercial realities of their own decisions.

Inspiration

+ Develop your own world class strategy to drive your business forward. Read *Playing to Win: How Strategy Really Works* by Alan Lafley and Roger Martin.[37] This manual for strategy practitioners outlines a practical framework for developing strategic goals, which has been successfully applied at leading brands such as Olay, Bounty, Gillette and Pampers.

+ Extend your understanding of emerging economic issues by downloading regular podcasts from the BBC's 'The World of Business', featuring content from the BBC World Service and BBC Radio 4's *In Business* programme. To gain a greater understanding of the world economy, try out investopedia.com – the world's leading source of financial content on the web, or listen to *Planet Money* podcasts, which provide easy-to-digest insights into key business trends.

+ Adopt a hedgehog. In his book *Good to Great*, Jim Collins studied twenty-eight successful organisations to find out what separated the good from the great.[38] Those who were able to identify their own 'hedgehog concept' – i.e. the one core aspect of their work to focus their energies on and do exceptionally well – were the ones who were more likely to beat their competitors and become highly profitable businesses. Read his classic book and undertake the three assessments needed to identify your own hedgehog concept.

+ Break from the pack. Create competitive advantage for your business through differentiation. Discover why this works and how to break free from the norm by reading *Different: Escaping the Competitive Herd* by Youngme Moon.[39]

 # Related work skills

Commitment to Change and Adaptation (3), Constructive Communication (4), Creativity and Innovation (5), Effective Planning and Organisation (7), Enthusiasm for Customer Service (8), Positive Decisions (15), Results through Action (18), Specialist Knowledge and Ability (19), Use of Information and Data (21).

Commitment to Change and Adaptation

Commitment to Change and Adaptation

People who are committed to change and adaptation apply lessons previously learned to new challenges. They encourage collaboration through the use of exceptional communication. Generally, they will be inclined to associate innovation and invention with new commercial possibilities and are comfortable navigating through complex and disruptive environments. They embrace change and development and are more likely to cope effectively during times of uncertainty. Great at reconciling conflicting priorities, these adaptive individuals have the capacity to help others to understand and deal with concerns relating to change. By responding positively to adaptation at work and acting as a change champion, they are able to encourage contribution from all.

Ideas for personal development

> *Don't spend time beating on a wall, hoping to transform it into a door.*
>
> **Coco Chanel**

Tools

- Focus your energy and attention on the things you can control. Refer to Stephen Covey's 'circle of influence'.[40] Be proactive and look to increase your own circle of influence.

Ask yourself these questions: do I understand the reason for the change? Do I agree with the reasoning? Do I believe I can cope? What will I gain? What will stay the same? What will I lose? If you can't answer these questions, ask someone who can.

Techniques

Recognise that all change starts with an ending – and that this can be an emotional experience as people begin to let go.

Get informed. Don't just sit and wait for information on changes at work; be proactive and seek out the information you need.

Change can cause anxiety and stress, so look after your health. Physical well-being is the bedrock of personal energy.

Give people time (but not too much time) to absorb what is happening. Be prepared for a drop in performance, morale and confidence in the short term.

Practise ways to present a calm and controlled demeanour during times of uncertainty. Seek support – change comes in all shapes and sizes. It is natural to feel a little overwhelmed if a lot happens at once.

Consider individual variables in terms of how people respond to change – age, psychological disposition, external stressors, life state and ability to deal with ambiguity all play a part.

Inspiration

Read *The Moment: Wild, Poignant, Life-Changing Stories from 125 Writers and Artists Famous and Obscure* by Larry Smith, and discover how turning points, epiphanies, unexpected coincidences and sudden catastrophes can all create life changing moments for us all.[41]

+ Remember behavioural change is hard – even if our life depends on it. It has been estimated that 90 per cent of heart bypass patients fall back into their old habits after two years. Read Alan Deutschman's book *Change or Die* to discover a three-part strategy for beating these odds, and learn a thing or two about change management in the process.[42]

⚙ Ideas for delivering results

> *Notice that the stiffest tree is most easily cracked, while the bamboo or willow survives by bending with the wind.*
>
> **Bruce Lee**

Tools

▪ Complete an updated version of Julian Rotter's Locus of Control questionnaire and consider how your results may impact on your ability to embrace change.[43]

▪ Generate multiple solutions. Fixating helps the brain to cope with uncertainty but prevents us from solving problems.[44] Search online for the 'cheap necklace problem' exercise to find out how fixating on a single solution at the expense of other alternatives can impair our ability to move forwards.[45]

▪ Apply a little neuroscience to support your colleagues during change. Look into David Rock's SCARF model and use this simple tool to minimise perceived threats and maximise rewards during times of change.[46]

▪ Consider how technology could assist – but remember OO + NT = EOO (Old Organisation + New Technology = Expensive Old Organisation). Technology is only one lever and people must come first.

■ Focus on the planning process, not the plan. Look into using 'brown paper planning' as a method to prepare your projects and increase your chances of success. It helps to engage your team in the planning process and builds ownership of implementation.

Techniques

▲ Recognise that developing self-awareness and personal motivation are both key to supporting yourself and others during change. Acknowledge that resistance can come from a combination of emotional, rational and political drivers.

▲ Support yourself and others by understanding all the stages of the change cycle.[47] Provide people with what they need during each of the five stages of transition – denial, anger, bargaining, depression and acceptance. Be aware people may move through these stages at different rates and may sometimes slip backwards.

▲ Develop a reputation for being someone who demonstrates an appetite for new knowledge. This will help you to anticipate any future changes and send out a message to others that you are adaptable and responsive.

▲ Help others to accept the change by creating certainty during uncertain times. Achieve this by being open and transparent about what is happening, accentuating the positive aspects of the change, celebrating any short-term wins and acting on all feedback received.

▲ As the change approaches, try to acknowledge the things you used to be able to do but can't do now, and the things you couldn't do before but can do now. As change unfolds, identify the things you used to do and still can, and the things you couldn't do before and still can't.

▲ Get yourself actively involved in the change – join new workgroups and empower yourself by influencing the outcomes.

▲ Discuss the consequences of the following statement by Richard Beckhard with your colleagues: 'People do not resist change; they resist being changed.'

▲ Develop your in-house capability. Identify change ambassadors who are both inquisitive and enthusiastic.

▲ Acknowledge the knowing–doing gap. You are unlikely to motivate anyone unless you can get them to feel confident about their ability first, so allow them to practise small parts of the change first.

Inspiration

✦ Monitor any inclination towards always wanting to get things 100% right. Good is usually good enough. Highly conscientious people have the strongest correlation with change resistance. Sensitise yourself to the subtle dangers of this form of self-critical mindset by reading *Finish: Give Yourself the Gift of Done* by Jon Acuff.[48] It is full of concrete actions to help you overcome this pervasive barrier to progress and begin to start moving forwards again.

✦ Adopt an adaptive mindset. Read *Adaptability: The Art of Winning in an Age of Uncertainty* by Dr Max McKeown and learn how to differentiate between adapting to cope and adapting to succeed.[49] This short management handbook is packed with practical advice and real-life examples to illustrate the importance of building operational flexibility in a fast changing world.

✦ Reflect on Eckhart Tolle's observation, 'The most rigid structures, the most impervious to change, will collapse first'[50] – and consider whether this is also true of people.

✦ Encourage collaborative effort during periods of transition. Show colleagues *Lead India – The Tree* on YouTube.[51]

✦ Invest in a copy of *Switch: How to Change Things When Change is Hard* and read it from cover to cover.[52]

✦ Step back in time, buy some popcorn and watch *Desk Set* (1957), with Spencer Tracy; or if you prefer your change films more modern, try Brad Pitt in *Moneyball* (2011).

 # Ideas for long-term gain

> *Your success in life isn't based on your ability to simply change. It is based on your ability to change faster than your competition, customers, and business.*
>
> **Mark Sanborn**

Tools

- Introduce John Kotter's eight-step change model to generate a sense of urgency, and provide clarity in terms of which activities need to be undertaken when, to help you to make any change stick.[53]

- Use the RACI matrix to identify roles and responsibilities during an organisational change process – Responsible, Accountable, Consulted and Informed.[54]

Techniques

- Communicate in abundance during change. Concentrate on translating strategy into simple everyday language. Evaluate the impact of your communications. Gather feedback and conduct regular reviews.

- Build human stories to help communicate the change. Explain how the change came about, why the situation exists and offer a clear picture of the desired future state.

- Apply the simple principle that the greater the degree of change, the greater the degree of employee involvement required in order to build their commitment.

- Improve access and incentives for idea generation during decision making.

- Balance people and organisational concerns by applying Jeff Hiatt's ADKAR model to support change and manage both dimensions in tandem – Awareness, Desire, Knowledge, Ability and Reinforcement.[55]

- Be courageous and stick to your guns. Managing change can be both tough and unpopular. Recognise and reward people who are helping to make the change happen. Invest time and energy encouraging your change heroes, not your change saboteurs.

Inspiration

- Find out how to create a business which can flourish during relentless change and ferocious competition by reading *What Matters Now* by Gary Hamel.[56] It suggests practical ways to build innovation from the ground up.

- Deliver lasting change by focusing on human habits, not systems or processes. Learn why many people and companies struggle to change, while others seem to reinvent themselves overnight, by reading *The Power of Habit* by Charles Duhigg.[57]

 # Related work skills

Ability to Influence (1), Commercial Thinking (2), Creativity and Innovation (5), Direction and Purpose (6), Effective Planning and Organisation (7), Motivation to Succeed (12), People Management and Leadership Potential (14), Resilience and Emotional Control (17), Use of Information and Data (21).

Constructive Communication

Constructive Communication

People who communicate in a constructive way engage others through purposeful dialogue. They consult widely and develop lasting connections. By asking questions, they actively encourage feedback and then act on it. Great communicators seek first to understand. They are curious about what people have to say and are able to build rapport by making those around them feel valued. These individuals express themselves using appropriate language, pitch and tone and also recognise the importance of non-verbal communication. Generally, they manage the message to suit the audience and are able to leverage a range of digital solutions when sharing information. They are inclined to keep their explanations simple, ensuring that accuracy, brevity and clarity are key considerations.

 ## Ideas for personal development

> *First learn the meaning of what you say, and then speak.*
>
> **Epictetus**

Tools

- Good questions encourage better communication. Use open questions to expand what is being said and closed questions to confirm your understanding. Be bold and consider getting a henna tattoo of the names of Rudyard Kipling's 'six honest serving men' from his poem 'The Elephant's Child' – What, Why, When, How, Where, Who. Position it somewhere visible.

■ Keep your communication as simple as ABC – be Accurate, Brief and Clear. Be still and have one conversation at a time. Look people in the eye and give them your undivided attention.

Techniques

▲ Paraphrase and restate what others have said to demonstrate your understanding. Better still, acknowledge what the other person is feeling to show that you empathise: 'So what you are saying is you feel … because …'

▲ When working with new people, underline the message that you are on the same team. Use words like 'we', 'us', 'we're', 'our' and 'ourselves' to build a bond and remind everyone that you are all working together.

▲ Be brief in emails. Acknowledge receipt and reply with what you expect to happen in the subject line – for example: 'FOR INFO – new build completes on Tuesday'.

▲ Take responsibility for your comments by using 'I' statements. Say what you would like to happen. Be more assertive by clearly expressing your opinions and feelings calmly and with conviction, but without trampling over the rights of others.

▲ Learn to say no when required. Acknowledge the request, say no, then give your reasons.

Inspiration

✦ First seek to understand, then to be understood. Talk less and listen more. Find out how by reading *Time to Think* by Nancy Kline[58] and *The Lost Art of Listening* by Michael Nichols.[59]

✦ Ask more. Learn to cultivate trust by asking a greater number of people for help and assistance. Discover how this works by picking up a copy of *The Art of Asking: How I Learned to Stop Worrying and Let People Help* by Amanda Palmer.[60]

✦ Watch Adam Galinsky's TED Talk on 'How to Speak Up for Yourself'.[61] Find out how to assert yourself, navigate difficult social situations and expand your personal impact.

Ideas for delivering results

> *... regardless of the changes in technology, the market for well-crafted messages will always have an audience.*
>
> **Steve Burnett**

Tools

▨ Apply Friedemann Schulz von Thun's four-ears model and learn how to tune in to communication with an emphasis on facts, relationships, personal disclosure and/or appeals.[62]

▨ Convey complex messages using LIONS – apply Language which is easily understood, Isolate one topic, Organise your thoughts, Narrow the topic to key points and always Summarise.

▨ Find out about the PechaKucha method and learn how to give a brilliant, high impact presentation on any subject in less than seven minutes. Refine your delivery skills by presenting to increasingly larger audiences and asking for feedback.

▨ When meeting new people, ask insightful questions and learn their story. Have deeper conversations and build connections by downloading a free copy of the Proust Questionnaire. Alternatively, to build trust and develop interpersonal rapport, try out Arthur Aron's thirty-six questions to develop interpersonal closeness.[63] This battery of insightful questions has been shown to strengthen the bond between people and can accelerate a willingness to be open in just forty-five minutes.

▨ Use the PIP framework for better business presentations. Firstly, state the Purpose of the presentation, and then share why the presentation is important by outlining the Implications. Finally, provide a Preview of the topics to be discussed. The model offers a way to get people excited and on the same page about your presentation in less than a minute by clarifying expectations.

Techniques

▲ Request feedback on your own performance as often as possible: 'Am I being clear?', 'What would improve this report?' Set a goal to ensure that every workplace conversation makes a difference – that something happens as a result (even if this is simply strengthening an existing relationship).

▲ Avoid defensiveness, one of the greatest blockages to effective communication. Step back if you feel yourself becoming defensive and consider if it is possible you may be wrong. How do you know that your reality is the truth?

▲ Practise simplifying elaborate ideas. Answer the question, 'What is a flame?', in a way an eleven-year-old would understand and be interested in, then ask six of your colleagues to do the same and listen to their responses.

▲ Apply deliberate use of positive phraseology with work colleagues (but be sincere): 'What I can do for you is …', 'How can we get round this problem?', 'Certainly!', 'I have a solution', 'I can confirm that …', 'You can be confident in …'

▲ When planning to communicate to groups, forget about appealing to the intellect and focus on your intention first. Consider how you want to make others feel: do you want to inspire them, to excite them, to reassure them? Always build your message around your intention, then take them on a journey.

▲ Edit the number of words you use. Padding weakens statements and confuses the listener. Only when you say what you want can you say it with conviction.

▲ Watch out for the 'J' word. Always be respectful, but try to avoid overusing the word 'just': 'I just wanted to see it was okay if …', 'Just wondering if you'd decided on which of the …' Taking the 'J' word out of your sentences almost always clarifies the message and strengthens your position. Some observers suggest that women use this apologetic word more than men do.[64]

▲ Avoid using 'you' statements when attempting to influence the behaviour of others. 'You ruined my jacket' is aggressive, while 'I feel upset when you don't take care of my things' is not.

▲ Observe your own body language as well as that of others. Resist jumping to conclusions by trying to identify areas of incongruence between what is being said and the way it is said. Watch Amy Cuddy's TED Talk and see how 'Your Body Language May Shape Who You Are'.[65]

▲ Monitor the social trend for two-way conversation to be replaced by personal broadcasting. Tune in to the subtle, to the understated.

▲ Deal with any individual performance concerns of others at the earliest possible stage, beginning informally through the use of honest conversations. Focus on behaviour, not personality, when providing feedback – be descriptive, not judgemental.

▲ If you have to hold meetings, make them magical. Look for unusual places to convene your important gatherings. Try out historic sites, local museums, universities or other places which take people away from their usual work environment. Finish every meeting with three simple questions: (1) What do we need to do now? (2) Who's going to do it? and (3) What is the deadline for this task? Using these three questions will mean something always happens after each magical meeting is over.

Inspiration

✛ Buy a copy of *The Power of Communication* by Helio Fred Garcia.[66]

✛ Become a better public speaker. Pick up great tips from *The Lost Art of the Great Speech* by Richard Dowis.[67] Find new ways to structure your message, improve your delivery and maximise the power of language.

✛ Gorge yourself on the 2014 film *Chef,* with Jon Favreau. Then acknowledge some of the less savoury aspects of what can happen if you unknowingly mismanage your digital footprint.

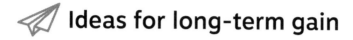 # Ideas for long-term gain

> *If you can't explain it simply, you don't understand it well enough.*
>
> **Anon.**

Tools

▪ Recognise your preferred communication style during conflict by completing the Thomas–Kilmann Instrument (TKI).[68]

▪ If you are tasked with convincing a group of people, try using the Bottom Line Up Front (BLUF) approach. State how they will benefit from the material early on and use the rest of your presentation to explain the how and the why. Use stories and anecdotes to explain the important points.

▪ Use the S-curve technique when presenting to large groups to create the illusion that you are looking at every single person in the room. Begin with the person sitting at the back on the right hand side and then move your gaze through the crowd in an S-shaped manner until you come to the person at the front left hand side.

Techniques

▲ When delivering bad news, try the inoculation technique to keep people on board. This involves getting people prepared for what is coming by using phrases such as, 'Right, now I'm going to share a really tough piece of advice …' or 'I've some bad news for you that I'd like you to listen to …'

▲ Next time you need to prepare for a challenging 'honest conversation' with someone, create a no-compromise statement and be clear of the one thing which must change moving forwards.

▲ Expose destructive behaviours in others by highlighting your area of concern. Use 'When you … (behaviour) it made me feel … (impact)', then immediately afterwards say, 'Is this (outcome) what you meant to achieve?' and wait for their response.

▲ Try speaking more extemporaneously in meetings. Expressing yourself with little or no preparation takes practice, but it can promote a more natural communication style which will assist with audience engagement and provide you with the flexibility to respond to the questions and responses of others. Find out more by reading *Improv Wisdom: Don't Prepare, Just Show Up* by Patricia Ryan Madson.[69]

▲ Go on the pull. Investigate the use of an ESN (Enterprise Social Network) to enable more 'pull' communications in the workplace. Help remote and virtual team members to digitally access and contribute information at their discretion and around their own schedules.

Inspiration

✛ Identify opportunities to reframe negative statements. An angry dad drags his teenage daughter in to see a counsellor. He says, 'She's too headstrong! She never listens to me and she won't do as she's told!' The counsellor replies, 'Isn't it wonderful that when she grows up she'll be able to stand on her own two feet and no one will get the better of her?'

✛ Consider the direct connection between how people feel and the methods of communication they use. Italian research published in *PLOS ONE* confirms that we all have definitive communication preferences which are shaped by our personality, and we will tend to become more stressed if we have to operate outside our preferred channels for long periods.[70]

Related work skills

Ability to Influence (1), Commercial Thinking (2), Direction and Purpose (6), Enthusiasm for Customer Service (8), Interpersonal Awareness and Diplomacy (10), People Management and Leadership Potential (14), Teamwork and Collaboration (20), Use of Information and Data (21).

Constructive Communication

KEY 5

Creativity and Innovation

Creativity and Innovation

People who adopt a creative mindset look beyond the first right answer by generating a range of alternative approaches and ideas. Typically, they can identify imaginative solutions and will question traditional assumptions. These individuals are able to uncover different avenues and opportunities when faced with unfamiliar situations. They make connections between ideas and are likely to recognise patterns and relationships. Curious by nature, they can suspend judgement and tolerate ambiguity in the workplace. More inclined to solve problems through collaborative enterprise, they are likely to be a catalyst for the introduction of new possibilities and directions. Capable of combining a number of established approaches to create innovative solutions, they will often focus on the practical application of novel ideas.

Ideas for personal development

> *You can't use up creativity. The more you use, the more you have.*
>
> **Maya Angelou**

Tools

- Capture all your ideas – write things down. As soon as we have over five or six items on our mind, things begin to drop off and be lost. Use popular apps such as Evernote to make sure you never forget an important idea.

■ Micro-manage. Microfiction is a form of writing which involves developing ultra-short stories of only 100 to 300 words. The approach allows you to develop your creativity skills through the creation of simple narratives without having to set scenes or build character. There are lots of online microfiction groups you can join, such as 100wordstory.org, to receive feedback on your work and encourage your inner creative. If you struggle with the process of writing, try out one of the many writing productivity apps, such as Prolifiko, to set goals and track your progress.

Techniques

▲ Be an observer of everyday problems. Define each problem as clearly as you can – be specific. Identify potential causes, then look for possible solutions.

▲ Read as much as you can (exercise the brain), read as little as you can (rest the brain). Back and forth. Back and forth. When exercising, pick up a copy of *A Technique for Producing Ideas* by James Webb Young to help you develop some original solutions.[71]

▲ Learn to be child-like (not childish). Play more and defer decision making for as long as possible. Embrace the principle that if at first the idea is not absurd, then there is no hope for it.

▲ Relax – use displacement activities. Stretch and relax like a concertina. Exercise can boost original thought patterns and help you to come up with a greater number of solutions to problems. Try new experiences and undertake new challenges to promote creativity. Change your environment and physiology to see things in a new way.

▲ Recognise that your rational, logical brain is slower to wake in the morning, so spend the first few minutes of every day in a state of relaxed attention and see if you can generate new ideas. Try using Julia Cameron's Morning Pages ritual to get your creative juices flowing by writing down longhand three uncensored pages of whatever comes into your mind shortly after you wake each morning.[72]

▲ Be sarcastic. This sounds too crazy to work, but it has been found that the dual meanings found in sarcasm can actually increase your ability to solve creative problems.[73]

Inspiration

✛ Watch Elizabeth Gilbert's TED Talk 'Your Elusive Creative Genius'.[74] When you know where your creative genius lives, discover how to foster more of it by watching the most popular TED Talk of all time, 'Do Schools Kill Creativity?' by Sir Ken Robinson.[75]

✛ Listen to classical music. While the 'Mozart effect' may only be beneficial to children and developing brains, classical music fires many more synapses in the brain than popular music and may help you to relax.[76] Try out some baroque music such as Vivaldi's *The Four Seasons* or Pachelbel's 'Canon' to get your creative juices flowing.

⚙⚙ Ideas for delivering results

The other day I was walking my dog around the building on the ledge. Some people are afraid of heights. Not me, I am afraid of widths.

Stephen Wright

Tools

▣ Go on a Six Hats Thinking course by the de Bono Group – or better still, train to become an accredited practitioner and teach others how to use a variety of different approaches to solve everyday business problems.[77]

- Use SCAMPER as a checklist for asking questions and testing assumptions.[78] This activity-based thinking process is an acronym to help people think of unusual ideas. It involves asking the following questions: how can I Substitute this product, problem or process? Combine it? Adjust it? Modify it? Put it to other uses? Eliminate it? Rearrange it?

- Never forget an idea. Verbalising your goals helps your brain to process information in a different way. Alternatively, send voice notes to your colleagues using an app like Braintoss in just two taps.

Techniques

- Emphasise quantity over quality. Avoid adopting the first expedient solution to a problem. Look for the third, the ninth, the sixteenth. Fill your bucket with as many unlikely ideas as you can. Ask – the way you ask the question determines the answer you get. Keep asking why. Ask for more ideas, more images, more alternatives.

- Compartmentalise your thinking. Copy Walt Disney, who used three different rooms for three different processes: the dreamer room, the realist room and the spoiler/critic room. Three separate steps at separate times, with no overlap.

- Become a peripatetic. Follow Aristotle's lead and practise thinking while you walk. Search out behavioural scientist Marily Oppezzo's five-minute TED Talk entitled 'Want to Be More Creative? Go for a Walk' to discover simple steps you can take to harness the power of walking to enhance your creativity.[79]

- Become a beginner – learn something new like hula hooping, wood carving or dancing, or why not try out a new language for free at duolingo.com. Practise your drawing skills. Sketching an idea is often more natural than writing. Envisage how your problem may look at a future desired state – draw what this would look like.

- Use the random entry method to stimulate new thinking. By applying unconnected input you can open up new lines of thinking. Gather unexpected stimuli using nouns from any book by opening random pages, then use each word selected blindly to create associations with your current challenge. Identify other random words and repeat.

- Apply the reversal technique. What factors would make your problem worse? Next, reverse these to identify ways to improve the situation.

- Practise not knowing. The first ideas we come up with are usually based on memories – ordinary ideas we are familiar with that can be tweaked. Creative ideas usually require additional input. Mix it up. Get someone else's opinion. Being around people who are unfamiliar and different to us makes us more innovative, diligent and harder-working.

- Use obstacles to improve performance. People recall more of what they have read when it is printed in smaller, less legible type.[80] Sometimes we need disruption to solve the problem.

- Try sticking to a strict schedule. Most creative minds religiously schedule their time. Ernest Hemingway rose at 6am every day and worked solidly until his midday break. Psychologist William James observed that an effective schedule allows us to 'free our minds to advance to really interesting fields of action'.

- Read more – acquire knowledge, ideas and strategies. In *The Miracle Morning*, Hal Elrod recommends reading just ten pages per day.[81] This only equates to about ten to fifteen minutes of reading in twenty-four hours, yet adds up to 3,650 pages or around eighteen books a year! Make your reading count by making a note of two things: lessons learned and any new commitments you will make.

- Compare the creativity levels of others by using the alternative uses test. How many uses can they think of for various inanimate objects in two minutes – a drawing pin, a razor blade, a toilet roll?

- Think *inside* the box. Imposing seemingly unreasonable constraints can often inspire greater creativity. Dr. Seuss found that setting limits to his work led to one of the most popular children's books in history. *Green Eggs and Ham* was the result of a bet that he wouldn't be able to write a book using only fifty words. He replicated this approach for other books – *The Cat in the Hat* was written using only first grade vocabulary. Creating boundaries can sometimes stop you drowning in a sea of possibilities.

▲ Take it lying down. Evidence suggests that our ability to solve creative problems may actually increase when we are flat on our back.[82] Researchers at the Australian National University discovered that volunteers were faster at solving anagrams lying down as compared to when they were standing. Warning: long-term use of this unconventional strategy may prove to be counterproductive, especially if you are feeling sleepy!

▲ Leave something undone. At the end of the day, leave a problem slightly unfinished so your subconscious mind can work on it overnight.

Inspiration

✛ While silence is best for focus, ambient noise levels (not loud) have been found to improve creative thinking.[83] Brian Eno's *Music for Airports* is often cited as one of the best examples of ambient music.

✛ Grab a copy of *Originals* by Adam Grant and discover how non-conformists move the world: 'Being original doesn't require being first. It just means being different and better.'[84]

✛ Be a little boring. In her book *Bored and Brilliant*, Manoush Zomorodi suggests the more times we have to switch our attention, the higher our stress levels go.[85] Instead, switch off, get bored and discover your most brilliant ideas. Watch her TED Talk 'How Boredom Can Lead to Your Most Brilliant Ideas' to learn how this works.[86]

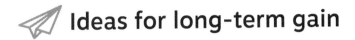 # Ideas for long-term gain

> *Creativity is thinking up new things. Innovation is doing new things.*
>
> **Theodore Levitt**

Tools

- Fuse ideas – things that don't normally go together. Invest in a Creative Whack Pack by Roger Von Oech or a set of Oblique Strategies by rock producer Brian Eno. Both decks of cards encourage you to look at things from a different viewpoint.

- Tap into collective intelligence and gather multiple ideas. InnoCentive is one example of an open innovation and crowdsourcing website.

Techniques

- Challenge the notion that creativity is a single thing – a moment of blinding inspiration. Eureka moments are very rare. Most great ideas are cobbled together and require preparation and persistence.

- Trial and error usually triumphs. Real-world research and rapid prototyping has consistently been found to be more successful than leaving creativity to the lone genius.

- Learn to suspend judgement and tolerate ambiguity. The ability to embrace paradoxes can increase creativity levels. Test yourself by checking out the Epimenides paradox,[87] and then help your colleagues to acknowledge that contradicting concepts can often complement each other.

- Widen the spectrum. PayPal founder Peter Thiel makes a point of deliberately hiring staff with autism and Asperger's to encourage the exploration of more innovative ideas – thus reducing the potential for what he calls 'herd-like thinking'.

▲ Netflix and chill. Traditional hierarchical cultures may disenfranchise people and stifle levels of innovation. Emulate the successes of organisations like Netflix and Spotify by making it easier for employees to develop and action new ideas by introducing flatter structures with fewer management levels.

▲ Parade creative ideas and reward others for innovative practices. Demonstrate an enthusiasm for innovation in the team.

Inspiration

✦ Buy or blag a copy of *Thinking, Fast and Slow* by the Nobel Prize winning Daniel Kahneman.[88]

✦ Forget about brainstorming. New research suggests that the adoption of a 'no idea is a bad idea' approach may actually stifle creativity.[89] As an alternative, watch Linda Hill's TED Talk on 'How to Manage for Collective Creativity' to help you develop a 'marketplace of ideas' by focusing on constructive debates.[90]

 # Related work skills

Commercial Thinking (2), Commitment to Change and Adaptation (3), Effective Planning and Organisation (7), Intuitive Thought (11), Motivation to Succeed (12), Positive Decisions (15), Results through Action (18), Specialist Knowledge and Ability (19), Teamwork and Collaboration (20).

Direction
and Purpose

Direction and Purpose

People who instil a sense of direction and purpose communicate a clear vision of a desired future state. They are able to clarify the expected contributions of others and are likely to create goals and targets which are consistent with organisational intentions. They excel at defining key milestones for success and are able to break down complex goals into well-defined, short-term activities. Firm in purpose, they regularly review existing performance levels against agreed objectives.

 ## Ideas for personal development

> *Happiness is essentially a state of going somewhere, wholeheartedly, one-directionally, without regret or reservation.*
>
> **William H. Sheldon**

Tools

- Test AMS. Most people know about SMART goals (Specific, Measurable, Achievable, Realistic, Time-based), and while this can be a useful model for testing the robustness of an established goal, it is often less effective for helping to create a new goal. If you struggle to construct objectives which add value, apply AMS and make it easier to achieve a tangible outcome. Start with the Activity to be undertaken by using a verb – what needs to happen. Decide on how this activity will be Measured – how you know it has been completed. Finally, introduce a Standard – explaining to what degree or what quality it needs to be delivered.

■ Visit vinehouse.com and receive regular hints and tips on creating effective goals by signing up to their infrequent newsletters.

Techniques

▲ Apply simple rules when creating objectives and communicating expectations. Identify the expected results associated with each activity. Always provide the context for the task to be undertaken and check the other person's understanding.

▲ Before you consider providing direction to others, step back and reflect on where you fit in, where you are heading and what fires you up. Write down your responses and acknowledge that these may be different to those of your peers.

▲ Break down complex goals into clearly defined activities and extend ownership by encouraging personal accountability. Without collaboration in the creation of goals it is harder to gain commitment, so involve people at all stages of the goal setting process.

▲ Acknowledge that goals work – but only sometimes, so define each one carefully. Create aspirational goals which are achievable or they will have the opposite effect to the one intended. Research reveals that people who, for example, miss a savings goal are more likely to overspend afterwards.[91] Similarly, students who miss an assignment deadline are far more likely to never complete it all. Goals should be stretching but not too stretching.

Inspiration

✦ Hold on tight to your dream. Read Viktor Frankl's *Man's Search for Meaning* to discover the significance of his quote: 'A man who becomes conscious of the responsibility he bears toward a human being who affectionately waits for him, or to an unfinished work, will never be able to throw away his life. He knows the "why" for his existence, and will be able to bear almost any "how".'[92]

- If you don't know your passion, reassure yourself that you are not alone and watch Terri Trespicio's TEDx Talk 'Stop Searching for Your Passion'.[93]

- March to your own beat. Take inspiration from Ray Charles' fifty-year career by watching the exuberant musical biopic *Ray* (2004). Have confidence in your sense of purpose and learn ways to stay true to it – even in the face of adversity.

- Develop a design for life. Treat yourself to a business bestseller. Order a copy of *Designing Your Life: How to Build a Well-Lived, Joyful Life* by Bill Burnett and Dave Evans and find out how you can create a life in which you can thrive – whatever your age or circumstance.[94]

⚙ Ideas for delivering results

> *It is more important to know where you are going than to get there quickly. Do not mistake activity for achievement.*
>
> **Mabel Newcomber**

Tools

- Research the results provided by OKRs in terms of helping to foster a sense of purposeful direction. Objective Key Results are now used by Google, Spotify and LinkedIn as a way of measuring/improving performance. Each individual sets their own objective for the next three months. They are freely shared across the organisation, yet not connected to rewards or performance ratings, making everyone more collaborative.

- Use the three letter test. Ask *why*. Reinforce your organisational mission statement by asking your people *why* they are doing what they are doing. Ask them *why* they are working on this particular project. Probe each response; ultimately, answers should link back to the wider purpose.

Techniques

▲ Take Dale Carnegie's advice and be responsible for giving those around you 'a fine reputation to live up to'.[95] People rise to high expectations – it boosts their confidence and makes them feel their goals are obtainable. Inspire others by painting an aspirational view of the future which they can relate to and contribute towards.

▲ Be firm in purpose. Seek to identify key themes and recurring patterns in the performance of the team or department and use this data to extend the results of others.

▲ Be resilient. Demonstrate to others that you respond well to challenging goals and objectives.

▲ Reflect on what fires you up – what you love to do most. Find out the same about your team members. What is their passion outside of work? What are their deep interests? Are there any overlapping themes with their existing work content? Look for innovative ways to integrate their passions in ongoing work projects when applicable.

▲ Acknowledge that flexible approaches to the work–life balance can improve retention rates and job satisfaction, helping people to progress with purposeful goals.

▲ Apply the progress principle to build a sense of purpose in others. Studies suggest that nothing is more motivating than progress in meaningful work – a sense of steady movement towards an important goal.[96] Once established, encourage your colleagues to share their goals across teams to develop their understanding of interdepartmental priorities and aspirations.

▲ Align and engage. Ensure all your one-to-ones and feedback sessions with team members include a conversation to check that each person knows what to do and has the desire to see it through. Apply a flexible and adaptive approach to the monitoring and reviewing of progress. Remember, intellectual engagement is often less powerful than emotional engagement.

▲ Show enthusiasm for the task and confidence in the person. Build motivation by conducting regular reviews and providing feedback which is clear and summarises precisely what you expect from others.

- Consider undertaking a purpose review as part of any performance review process to help identify what other people see as important. Recognise overlapping themes and consider if these can be replicated.

- Provide a clearer line of sight between each role and the wider organisational plans by applying a three-pronged approach. Firstly, stress the priorities – because everyone wants to know what to expect and what to do. Secondly, remind everyone about their individual and team goals – the reason the priorities exist. Thirdly, emphasise how these tie into wider cultural norms and behavioural expectations. Making these elements explicit makes it more likely that the objectives will be realised.

- Be congruent. Compose goals in line with your declared organisational values. Be relatable. Express your goals from the end user's perspective.

- Engage your team by providing opportunities for personal coaching and training. Organise the work efficiently, taking time to listen by creating channels for the employee voice to be heard.

- Ask people if they had a good day, then if they did, ask them what it was that made it worthwhile. Try to work together to create more of these moments every day.

- Disassociate purpose and cause. Recognise that work isn't always about deciding on your 'true calling'. Purpose is simply an approach to work and serving others. You don't need to be working for a higher cause to have it. Purpose is about finding your direction, not deciding on your destination.

- Rip it up (or replace it with a meaningful one). A growing number of organisations are recognising that vision statements should be lived, not laminated. Abolish complex, rhetoric laden statements presented in a gilt frame in your reception area, and instead opt for a collaboratively created short, punchy slogan which captures what you do in one or two sentences.

Inspiration

+ Share the story of Captain D. Michael Abrashoff of the *USS Benfold* who transformed the fortunes of his first ever command, a guided missile destroyer, by committing to be the best: 'I decided *Benfold* was going to be the best damn ship in that Navy. I repeated it to my sailors all the time, and eventually they believed it themselves.'[97] His slogan for his 310 crew members was 'It's your ship'. Results on the *USS Benfold* skyrocketed because the crew felt they had greater ownership and believed what they were doing was important. In Abrashoff's first year, the vessel went from last to first, winning the Spokane Award for the top performing ship in the Pacific fleet.

+ Take a fresh look at *Life of Pi* by Yann Martel.[98] This unexpected tale of survival underlines the importance of believing in something – be it religion, the natural elements or your own personal strength.

+ Listen to the CIPD podcast by Philippa Lamb on the importance of creating and sustaining a sense of shared purpose. Hear all about the 'golden thread' and how it links to both employee motivation and improved performance.[99]

 # Ideas for long-term gain

> *One person with a belief is a social power equal to ninety-nine who have only interests.*
>
> **John Stuart Mill**

Tool

▪ Create a positive psychological climate to provide people with a sense of meaning. Take a look at Peter Warr's twelve environmentally centred elements and use this model to evaluate your own workplace.[100]

Techniques

▲ Be a good sport. Although there is no magic formula for success, a study of serial winning Olympic coaches who have excelled in their field suggests that 'driven benevolence' is the approach most likely to deliver continuous achievement. Typically, all of the super-coaches demonstrated 'a relentless and purposeful quest for self-improvement and victory' balanced with a genuine desire to 'considerately support oneself and others'.[101] Look into the research by Sergio Lara-Bercial and Clifford Mallett to find out how to balance these two requirements and instil a greater sense of purpose to elevate the performance of those around you.

▲ Assign the ends, but not the means. Decide on the destination, then allow your people to select the route.

▲ Be age appropriate by focusing on purpose, not profit. A recent survey by Deloitte revealed that millennials and younger people are much more attracted to organisations which can demonstrate how they contribute to wider society.[102]

▲ Acknowledge the disruptive influence of change on everyone's sense of direction and purpose. Draw people in by telling authentic stories – explain the change as a vivid human narrative. Define emerging opportunities and demonstrate your belief to make it seem possible. Be clear what will change and what will not. Build a sense of ownership as soon as possible by involving them in the change.

▲ Be sensitive to the communication needs of others during workplace transitions and prioritise tasks to ensure people are fully briefed during periods of significant upheaval.

▲ Empower people in your area to develop their own ways of working and make decisions for themselves within agreed boundaries. Strengthen their sense of direction by encouraging them to think in terms of increasingly longer timescales.

Inspiration

✦ Learn how great leaders inspire action by watching Simon Sinek's TED Talk entitled 'How Great Leaders Inspire Action'.[103]

- Enrich people's sense of purpose by following the lead of Google, Atlassian and 3M and allowing a proportion of time every week for staff to work on projects they find interesting.

- Be a culture vulture by swooping down on Firespring. Learn how their 'special sauce' has helped them to create a fun-loving workplace through the development of a shared sense of purpose. Pinch their own delicious recipe by watching Jay Wilkinson's TEDx Talk on 'Company Culture'.[104]

 # Related work skills

Ability to Influence (1), Commercial Thinking (2), Commitment to Change and Adaptation (3), Constructive Communication (4), Effective Planning and Organisation (7), People Management and Leadership Potential (14), Positive Decisions (15), Professional Ethics and Social Responsibility (16), Teamwork and Collaboration (20).

Effective Planning and Organisation

Effective Planning and Organisation

People who plan and organise work requirements in an efficient way manage resources and people to deliver outcomes on time and in full. These individuals think ahead. They manage time effectively, prioritise tasks and are able to work to deadlines. Often, they will follow systems and procedures and excel at working to a schedule. Great at coordinating tasks in a logical and systematic way, they are likely to monitor results, anticipate issues and delegate where appropriate. Capable of devising and implementing processes to achieve organisational goals, they will adjust plans and tasks to meet changing priorities.

 ## Ideas for personal development

> *Organising is what you do before you do something, so that when you do it, it is not all mixed up.*
>
> **A. A. Milne**

Tools

- Value time as a resource. Try using a Google productivity extension called StayFocusd. This allows you to set a time limit for sites you visit and sometimes get lost in. For example, you could set a fifteen-minute maximum daily setting for LinkedIn to make your visits to the site more effective.

Gain insight into the demands placed on your time. Put first things first by using Eisenhower's urgent–important matrix. Review all your tasks, map them on the matrix and rank each item. Place higher value items first, then integrate lower value items next. The momentary appeal of urgent tasks may seem irresistible; however, they can blindside us and absorb our energy.

Techniques

Start by understanding precisely what tasks need to be undertaken. Establish goals, set timelines and prioritise.

Ask three 'what?' questions of yourself. What is it that only I can do to make a difference? What are my highest value activities? What is the most valuable use of my time right now?

Recognise that busyness is not business. To-do lists may motivate (ticking off small tasks) but can mask larger concerns. Don't be tempted by the lure of easy implementation. Hardest tasks first is often a more helpful approach.

Take control. Have less stuff and simplify everything around you. If you have lots of competing priorities, then get visual. Divide your tasks, calendars and lists using your own colour coding system to enable you to differentiate between competing demands.

Combine the use of accountability, commitment and documentation during goal creation. Research from the Dominican University of California suggests that to accomplish your plans you should always write down your goals, formulate action plans and then build in accountability by sending regular progress reports to a colleague or friend.[105]

Spend thirty minutes at the weekend to prepare your plan for the week ahead. At the end of each work day (or in the evening), create a broad brush plan for the following day of work ahead. Plan your time, not your tasks. Devise activity chunks rather than minute-to-minute detail.

If, for some reason, things don't go according to plan and you are running late for a meeting, why not stop and pick up some coffees for everybody. You'll be a hero.

Inspiration

✣ Watch Stephen Covey's 'Put the First Things First' video and then listen to the full CD/MP3 of the same name.[106]

⚙ Ideas for delivering results

> *If I had eight hours to chop down a tree, I'd spend six sharpening the axe.*
>
> **Anon.**

Tools

▦ Download and use one of the many productivity apps available for most platforms. Simple task managers such as Google Keep, Wunderlist and Remember the Milk are easy to use and enable you to free up more mental space.

▦ Copy Leonardo da Vinci and create a 'master list'.[107] Put everything in one place – work and home. Include short-, medium- and long-term goals. Review this list twice a day.

▦ When planning the overall time required for any new project, check out PERT (Programme Evaluation and Review Technique). PERT can often provide an accurate estimate of the time required for each stage.

▦ Remember Parkinson's law – tasks will always stretch to the time allocated to them, so always put finish times as well as start times to any appointments and meetings.[108] Also share this with the other party to help manage expectations.

▦ Undertake an accredited Myers–Briggs Type Indicator assessment and consider the consequences of your own preferences. Are you more structured or more flexible in your approach to deadlines?

- Use business efficiency tools such as Dropbox, Evernote and Google Docs to manage, share and collaborate on work documents.

- When planning a project remember to factor in thinking time. Think on paper first and then apply Ockam's razor to slice through the problem.[109]

- Let it fade. If you're involved at the early stages of a project, introduce the FADE quality model to help minimise any risk of failure. Evaluating the Facts, Assumptions, Decisions and Execution of the planning process is a good place to start.

- During project planning, use Microsoft Project rather than buying expensive scheduling software. If some budget is available, consider saving time and making life easier by using Ganttic or Smartsheet.

Techniques

- Use goals to evaluate your progress and systems to make your target a reality. A goal may be to swim the English Channel, but the systems you introduce as a result of this intention are what will make it happen. Examples of systems might be to introduce a stretching new personal training plan, to begin eating healthier foods or to experiment using different swimming strokes.

- Take full responsibility for every single item on your task list or personal schedule. You have allowed everything that is there. If you use networked diaries such as Google Calendar, always allocate time in your diary for administrative tasks to prevent this time being reallocated by others for meetings and group work.

- Pay attention to what has your attention. Be aware of what your mind as well as your body is doing. Mind-wandering on the job reduces levels of personal effectiveness and satisfaction.[110]

- Recognise that multitasking isn't effective in the long run.[111] It takes longer to complete tasks, creates more errors and promotes poorer decision making. Where possible, do one thing at a time – brilliantly.

- Apply focus. Review your workload by looking at what can be eliminated, what can be automated, what can be delegated and then what can be actioned. Any deferred activities should be put through the same cycle.

- Limit interruptions by performing high priority tasks away from phones and emails. Turn off email alerts and cluster similar-themed activities together.

- Concentrate on the three 'Eff' words. Reflect on how you could make yourself more Effective (focus on the right things), Efficient (doing it in the right way) and Effortless (conserve your energy).

- Extend your personal confidence and capability by offering to organise aspects of the work and resources of others to maximise results. Volunteer to take responsibility for the scheduling of your next medium-sized project. Develop your skills by allocating time for specific tasks and assigning roles to certain employees.

- Bring the right people together. Involve the most relevant people in the plans and in the execution. Consider the use of an external facilitator when planning complex tasks.

Inspiration

- Get hold of a copy of *Getting Things Done* by David Allen and read it from cover to cover.[112]

- Discover the secrets of the incredibly well-organised by downloading Erik Fisher's award-winning podcasts available at beyondthetodolist.com. These include practical advice from successful people on building efficiency, optimising tasks, managing priorities and achieving balance.

# Ideas for long-term gain

> *The time to repair the roof is when the sun is shining.*
>
> **John F. Kennedy**

Tools

- Try a different approach. Burn Downs and Burn Ups provide accessible alternatives to Gantt charts. A burn down chart is more often used to represent activities with a shorter timescale, while a burn up chart is more suited to longer timescales where the projected work or activities may change.

- Find out more about using a Kanban board in your office to plan your own and your team's work tasks.[113] By applying this simple work visualisation tool you will be able to optimise the flow of your work. If you prefer a digital solution, why not try out Trello, which offers a free online version.

Techniques

- Chase opportunities to get more involved with long-term strategic planning, which may include market research, financial planning, budgeting and forecasting.

- Incorporate the voice of your customers in all your planning activities. Measure your ideas against the views of your end users.

- Develop a reputation for always asking 'What ifs'. Be the one who continually explores what is likely to happen if circumstances change. Encourage the adoption of pilot schemes and trial runs for higher risk large projects and events.

- Seek workable solutions by developing a long-term perspective. The solution-after-next principle involves identifying the perfect solution to a given problem and then working backwards to create practical short-term fixes – which will eventually become part of the ideal long-term solution.

- Review and simplify the current use of management controls in your area. Investigate options to make targets, performance standards, key performance indicators, budgets, procedures, schedules and record systems more easily embraced by adding flexibility.

- Don't over-plan strategic intentions. Attempting to nail down too many things in a bid to control long-term variables creates operational rigidity and overwhelms people.

- Apply the power of process. Try to think of everything as a process which can be broken down into stages, documented and replicated. Identify three of your own work practices which could be mapped out as a process. This will enable each task to be repeated with ease and, if appropriate, could also make them easier to be outsourced/delegated.

Inspiration

+ Check this out. Learn how to get organised by breaking down complex tasks into procedural checklists. Read *The Checklist Manifesto: How to Get Things Right* by Atul Gawande.[114] Discover how the introduction of simple steps can help you to reduce errors, increase operational efficiency, transform performance levels and create a culture of teamwork.

Related work skills

Commercial Thinking (2), Commitment to Change and Adaptation (3), Creativity and Innovation (5), Direction and Purpose (6), People Management and Leadership Potential (14), Positive Decisions (15), Results through Action (18), Specialist Knowledge and Ability (19), Use of Information and Data (21).

KEY 8

Enthusiasm for
Customer Service

Enthusiasm for Customer Service

People who have an enthusiasm for customer service seek to maintain positive personal contact with all their end users. They deal with customers in an engaging, professional and courteous way, listening to their requirements without making assumptions. Great at focusing on customer satisfaction levels, these individuals use client feedback as a key decision making consideration. They act as an ambassador for the organisation and will take responsibility for making improvements to services and work practices. They will demonstrate a deep understanding of customer needs and are likely to value loyalty and long-term commitment.

 ## Ideas for personal development

> *[Customers] are only interested in being able to get from you a product or service with the minimum of fuss and the maximum of convenience – their convenience.*
>
> **Simon Caulkin**

Tool

- Express your thanks. Go the extra millimetre by sending handwritten cards – they stand out, are appreciated and are very memorable.

Techniques

▲ Ignore everything you have ever been told about customer service. Do not treat customers how *you* would like to be treated – treat them how *they* would like to be treated. Practise active listening skills and admit your mistakes – even if you discover them before your customers do.

▲ Be informed and know your stuff. If a query is too complex or out of the scope of your role, know who to turn to and then make them easy for you to connect with.

▲ Resist standardising your offering too much, although agreeing a set of protocols for more routine areas (such as telephone greetings) may support a consistency of approach and help to manage expectations.

▲ Use clear communication featuring authentic, positive language. Remain composed and never end a conversation without confirming the customer is satisfied.

▲ Be empathetic, patient and consistent. Handle each individual differently, yet provide the same levels of service.

▲ Throw away the scripts and automated responses and treat customers as individuals. Concentrate on developing a reputation as being 'the person to ask for'.

▲ Get personal and be available. Customers want to feel they have access to real people. Provide physical addresses to build trust. Write timely responses to comments on social media postings and review sites.

▲ Know your customers' expectations and then exceed them to build loyalty and generate opportunities for repeat business. Feedback loops can help to signal where adjustments need to be made and will release you from the pressure of having to predict what is going to happen with every single aspect of your service delivery.

Inspiration

+ Where possible, personalise at least one aspect of your offering or allow your customer to make choices or decisions about how it is provided. Watch the short film *Johnny the Bagger* and see the impact one small action can make.[115]

⚙ Ideas for delivering results

> *Your most unhappy customers are your greatest source of learning.*
> **Bill Gates**

Tool

▦ Consider service delivery from a different angle using Strategyzer's Value Proposition Canvas. This simple tool for understanding your customers' needs can help you to design the products and services they really want. Search online to download a free copy.

Techniques

▲ Ensure your front entrances (physical and virtual) are impressive. These initial aspects are disproportionately important to your customers. They create lasting impressions and drive judgements about how they will be treated.

▲ Make everyone responsible for great customer service and, where possible, make one person accountable for it.

▲ Create short self-help videos to help your customers resolve common problems more quickly. Find one of the many online guides on how to produce these, then use a screen capture programme to produce your own in-house clips.

▲ Identify single customers to wow. Provide an experience so delightful that one lucky customer will have a great story to tell. Offer your own version of a free upgrade.

▲ Focus your energies on key touch points/moments of truth. Make sure the right skills are consistently demonstrated at every point where the customer has contact with someone from the organisation. Try to identify customer hot spots – or what Leah van Zelm calls SSBs (Single Selfish Benefits) – which are different for every customer. Identify these and focus on them to create stickiness. Visit merkleinc.com to read her blog on customer centricity.

▲ Spotlight random customers. Feature them on your website, in social media or in the team meeting. Let them know how much they mean to you.

▲ Visit your competitors regularly. Make trips to see examples of outstanding service and see what they do well. Hone in on behavioural aspects. Use secret users and mystery shoppers to test the user experience.

▲ Check the engagement levels of all your customer-facing staff. Use a simple engagement tool to make sure that you and your colleagues are both engaged and energised by your offering. Abolish empty slogans and posters saying things like 'Getting better together' and 'The customer is king'.

▲ Prevent interactions from becoming mundane by throwing in an occasional surprise element: an unexpected loyalty discount, tailored reward or service innovation which was not anticipated.

▲ Review all the ways your customers currently provide feedback. Make these more visible and more accessible, including use of contact pages, social media postings and comment cards at the point of service. Establish channels and build engagement one customer at a time.

▲ When dealing with complaints, where possible make sure that one person owns the customer case throughout the lifetime of the issue. If you want to know how to handle customer feedback on social media, discussion boards and review sites more effectively, pick up a copy of *Hug Your Haters* by Jay Baer and discover the best ways to embrace complaints, deal with online trolls and turn negative press into positive opportunities.[116]

- Always follow up with the customer after any problem is solved. This builds relationships and ensures the issue stays fixed.

- Acknowledge the fact that all staff will treat customers in the same way their boss treats them. Discuss the implications of this statement with your own line manager.

Inspiration

- Take time to reflect. Put your feet up and read *Delivering Happiness* by Tony Hsieh.[117]

- Be more principled. Invest in a copy of the award-winning *The Ten Principles Behind Great Customer Experiences* by Matt Watkinson.[118] It is full of practical advice which is easy to put into practice and works for any type of product or service.

- Get together with your colleagues and create a compelling customer position statement. Keep it very simple. Consider the Ritz-Carlton Hotel Company, who define themselves and their approach in just nine words: 'We are ladies and gentlemen serving ladies and gentlemen.'

- Act like you run a grocer's shop. Read Gary Vaynerchuk's *The Thank You Economy* and discover a heap of relevant ways to provide greater attention to your evolving customer experience by ensuring every single employee is comfortable engaging in authentic service.[119]

- Emulate retailers like B&Q and hire demographically diverse staff groups to whom customers can relate. Then empower them to be able to make decisions around resolving issues and providing discretionary discounts. Set limits on any reductions they can offer in order to manage your costs effectively.

- Purchase a recent edition of *The Richer Way* by Julian Richer.[120] Discover how to deliver great customer service by providing your team with the right training, support, appreciation and respect.

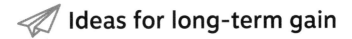 # Ideas for long-term gain

Tools

- Consider introducing NPS as a measure of customer relationships. Fred Reichheld's Net Promoter Score measures levels of loyalty between customer and provider, with higher scores linked to increased profitability.[121]

- Investigate the relevance of the old Tesco 'magic formula' of L2 (c + e) + r = s + p, and try to apply it to your team or organisation. According to David Fairhurst, former group resourcing director at Tesco, it means, 'listening a lot to our customers and employees plus responding accordingly equals sales and profitability'.[122]

Techniques

- Strive for internal and external alignment. Check that what is said through marketing and promotional vehicles matches what actually happens.

- Build human stories and campaigns by focusing on the experience, not the product or service. Let the customer know how it will look and feel to use your product/service. Consider virtual trials.

- Review all your existing customer relationship management systems. Use data mining techniques to pull customer information together. Apply a holistic view of the customer experience by aggregating data from social media, web analytics, customer buying history and in-store visits.

▲ Identify ways to turn any dissatisfied customers into loyal advocates through the use of an effective complaints management system. Introduce measures to improve response to core concerns such as time to resolution.

▲ Bring clusters of customers together to create customer communities. Build face-to-face user groups, webinars, trade shows and conventions. Establish focus groups, informal interviews and instant surveys to pick up on emerging customer needs. Seek opportunities for the customer to be able to control at least part of their own customer journey.

Inspiration

✢ Learn from online footwear giant Zappos and start every meeting with recent comments from a delighted customer or end user. Zappos also prides itself on establishing new records for the longest ever phone calls – because they want every customer to know they care about them and will spend whatever time is required to make them happy.

✢ Purchase a copy of *Webs of Influence* by Nathalie Nahai and uncover recent trends in consumer behaviour, plus ideas on how best to influence others using a profitable online strategy.[123]

✢ Be controversial and suggest that your organisation puts their employees first and customers second – but only after you've watched all of Vineet Nayar's TEDx Talk and discovered more about the long-term benefits of this approach.[124]

 # Related work skills

Ability to Influence (1), Commercial Thinking (2), Constructive Communication (4), Focus on Developing Others (9), Interpersonal Awareness and Diplomacy (10), Professional Ethics and Social Responsibility (16), Resilience and Emotional Control (17), Use of Information and Data (21).

KEY 9

Focus on Developing Others

Focus on Developing Others

People who focus on developing capability at work guide and support others through the creation of realistic opportunities for professional growth. They are committed to advancing the skills, knowledge and performance of those around them. As recognised supporters of a continuous learning environment, they balance the long-term aspirations of their colleagues with the needs of the organisation. They are likely to excel at introducing new ways to share knowledge and will encourage people to take ownership of their learning. Typically, they regard identified training needs as development possibilities. Capable of inspiring confidence in others, they are able to identify and celebrate the full range of diverse talents and abilities available in the workplace.

9

 ## Ideas for personal development

> *You cannot teach a man anything, you can only help him to find it within himself.*
>
> **Anon.**

Tools

■ Pick the right tools. Every year, the Centre for Learning Performance and Technologies compiles a comprehensive global summary of the 'Top 200 Tools for Learning'. This list delivers insights into the latest learning trends, methods for personal and professional development and unconventional options for workplace learning.

■ Abandon any reliance on old-fashioned learning styles questionnaires. They are easy to apply and very accessible, but are too restrictive and may lack both reliability and validity.[125]

Techniques

▲ Know your people. Collaborate to identify both skills and development areas. Explore long-term career aspirations. Challenge your team to take on responsibility for managing their own career management. Encourage them to reflect on their values, interests, aspirations, skills and temperament.

▲ Formulate robust learning and development plans for your whole team. Revisit and revise these intentions on a regular basis – don't just wait for formal performance review meetings. Be approachable and available.

▲ Engage your colleagues emotionally as well as rationally by co-creating objectives which appeal both to operational goals and their own career aspirations. When setting development goals for your people, try to balance identified needs across three themes – organisational, team and individual requirements.

▲ Be protective about time allocated to learning and development activities. Allocate, schedule and protect opportunities to extend capability.

▲ Develop people who are both willing and able. Always differentiate between commitment and capability performance requirements. While commitment can't always be taught, it can still be influenced.

▲ Apply carefully selected 'hinge questions' to informally underline key learning messages across your workgroup. Hinge questions can be used to underline pivotal moments or key thinking which you wish to highlight. For example, 'When do you think an administrator should forsake accuracy for speed?' may provoke a variety of interesting responses.

▲ Recognise that jobs are fluid and evolving and share your enthusiasm for developing the adaptive knowledge, skills and approaches of those around you. Demonstrate your own commitment to extending your capabilities through continual professional development.

Inspiration

✚ Reject conventional wisdom which says people can be fixed. Recent evidence reveals that your energies may be better invested in trying to draw out what has been put in, rather than wasting time attempting to address what has been left out.[126] Where possible, focus on strengths, not weaknesses.

 Ideas for delivering results

> *Never attempt to teach a pig to sing; it wastes your time and annoys the pig.*
>
> **Robert Heinlein**

Tools

▩ Throw out the old sandwich. The overused 'praise sandwich' technique (consisting of praise–criticism–praise) for providing feedback dilutes the message and is rarely effective.[127] Give positive feedback when the employee has earned it and negative feedback when it is necessary. Offering praise and criticism independently of one another is more respectful towards the employee and builds trust between you.

- Become a great coach to others. Use a simple framework like the GROW (Goal, Realities, Obstacles, Way forward) model and believe that time spent coaching your people is one of the most valuable activities you can undertake. Develop skills to unlock the potential of those around you by following the advice of Michael Bungay Stanier in his inspirational book *The Coaching Habit*.[128]

- Get into video. Using video to facilitate learning is now big business, with YouTube officially the number one web-based learning tool. Use screen casting and screen capture apps like Snagit, Camtasia and authoring tools like Articulate, Lectora, Adobe Captivate and Easygenerator to create great learning content.

- Watch the video 'How to Play Delegation Poker', then download a free copy of the cards from management30.com and use them as a participative exercise at your next team meeting.[129]

Techniques

- Develop your low commitment–low capability people by establishing boundaries and highlighting the standards expected. Invest in training, but be explicit about any unacceptable behaviour.

- Consider alternatives to formal training in situations where performance issues are a result of recruitment, selection or remuneration problems; policies and procedural issues; mismanagement; insufficient tools, equipment or resources; physical environment problems; or a lack of motivation.

- Encourage yourself and others to apply reflective practice. Think about what you did, what happened and what you would do differently next time.

- Add variety to your delivery options by including blended solutions where appropriate. Use e-authoring tools to create short, high impact sessions tailored to your own needs. Supplement this with immersive behavioural-based opportunities to practise skills and learn from others.

▲ Develop your low commitment–high capability people by making them feel more valued and rekindle their sense of purpose by getting them more connected with key tasks.

▲ Be receptive to unorthodox interpersonal development methods which may take place inside and outside the confines of the workplace. Drama simulations using professional actors such as forum theatre groups are useful for behavioural skills. Interventions such as Dialogue in the Dark, where employees participate in tasks in total darkness (or in total silence), can also be revealing.

▲ Develop high commitment–low capability people by encouraging them and providing them with further support. Recognise their contributions and strengthen their sense of belief.

▲ Develop your high commitment–high capability people by sharing important decision making with them and identifying new responsibilities.

▲ Recognise your key stakeholders. One of the main drivers of success for any investment in learning and development is the level of commitment provided by the line manager. Create an upward learning spiral by sharing the responsibility for developing employees between the manager, the individual and HR/L&D department.

▲ Delegate to develop others, not just to improve your personal efficiency. Identify the best person for the task and define the success measures you are expecting to see. Explore how much support and skills development is required. Provide the responsibility and authority to execute the task, but don't abdicate accountability.

Inspiration

✦ Cultivate individual growth. Sharpen your praise and positive encouragement by adopting a growth mindset. Foster more of what you want to see by praising the effort and approach, instead of focusing solely on the outcome and results. Read *Mindset: Changing the Way You Think to Fulfil Your Potential* by Dr Carol Dweck.[130]

- Mix up your traditional training methods. It doesn't all have to be classroom style delivery. Try out reading, participating, presenting, visiting, project involvement, empowerment, facilitating, buddying, role shadowing, professional studies, secondments, role enrichment, focus group membership, report construction and cross-functional awareness. Share some of the staff development podcasts available online, including: John Tomlinson's Trainer Tools interviews, audio readings of recent articles from ATD's *TD Magazine*, Learning Now Radio podcasts (part of Learning Now TV) and also the GoodPractice podcasts.

- Find out about the Dunning–Kruger effect, which states that unskilled individuals tend to mistakenly assess their ability to be higher than it actually is.[131] At the same time, highly skilled individuals tend to overestimate the relative capability levels of others by assuming that tasks which are easy for them will also be easy for their colleagues.

- Be there, be useful, be quick. Apply these three principles of Google's 'micro-moments' to your approaches to self-directed learning. Leverage emerging technologies to enable people to consume information through their mobile devices at a time convenient to them. Equip your staff to receive short, easy-to-access learning opportunities which are both quick and useful. Examples could include infographics, PDFs, gaming technologies, video clips and relevant articles.

- Discover the performance improvement effects obtained by combining clear goals with effective feedback by researching Albert Bandura's famous performance experiment with eighty cyclists.[132]

- Acknowledge the benefits of providing informal opportunities for people to learn and share good practice. Make it memorable by creating communities of learning. Find out one way to achieve this by watching John Green's TED Talk 'The Nerd's Guide to Learning Everything Online'.[133]

 # Ideas for long-term gain

> *… the ability to learn faster than competitors may be the only sustainable competitive advantage.*
>
> **Arie de Geus**

Tools

▪ Celebrate key learning and development successes by publicly parading the learning achievements of others. Promote your L&D provision internally and externally. Manage social media updates effortlessly using apps such as Buffer and HubSpot to share learning and development updates on social networks and pick up on the trends in your field.

▪ Create an adaptive learning environment. Check out Kerryn Kohl and Debbie Craig's SADEL model and learn how to build a sustainable Self-directed, Agile, Digital and Exponential Learning organisation.[134] Begin by developing methods to give learners more control over the 4P's of learning by focusing on Preference, Pace, Place and Path.

Techniques

▲ Be flexible in the adoption of the popular 70:20:10 model where 70 per cent of development comes through day-to-day tasks, 20 per cent through exposure to coaching, networking and collaboration, and 10 per cent through formal learning and professional qualifications. Fast-paced organisations and businesses going through large-scale transitions may need to turn this model on its head in the short term.

▲ Investigate the possibilities provided by an online learning management system or learning portal. These are beneficial for procedural, mandatory and knowledge-based learning, yet may be less useful for more behavioural-based learning.

9

Focus on Developing Others

▲ Champion a continuous feedback culture by involving peers and customers in the feedback loop.

▲ Re-evaluate your formal staff appraisal system. According to PwC, two-thirds of large companies are now rethinking their processes. Microsoft, Accenture and Deloitte have all dropped annual appraisal systems in favour of ongoing feedback.[135]

▲ Support higher performers. Stretch and challenge more able employees through job enlargement and job enrichment activities. Expand the performance threshold for your most talented people by providing them with self-directed learning projects to prevent them plateauing or from working mainly in their comfort zone.

▲ Invest in those who invest in others. Demonstrate organisational commitment to your learning practitioners by making their roles a springboard position into other, more senior managerial positions. Underline the importance of 'enabling the skills of others' during succession planning exercises. Bolster managerial capability and career planning by insisting all employees should have spent time in a people development or coaching role prior to being appointed into a managerial position.

Inspiration

✛ Drive the establishment of a mentoring network and oversee the matching of mentors and mentees across your team/ workgroup to bring about a long-term mentoring programme. Personally mentor other high potential staff. Musician Ray Charles mentored Quincy Jones, fashion designer Christian Dior mentored Yves St Laurent, Albert Einstein had Max Talmud. Later, consider opportunities for you to be guided by another person in a non-managerial role and investigate the benefits of a reverse mentoring arrangement.

✛ Anticipate future challenges and prepare effectively for impending labour shortages and skill gaps by watching Rainer Strack's TED Talk 'The Workforce Crisis of 2030 and How to Start Solving It Now'.[136]

Related work skills

Commitment to Change and Adaptation (3), Enthusiasm for Customer Service (8), Interpersonal Awareness and Diplomacy (10), People Management and Leadership Potential (14), Professional Ethics and Social Responsibility (16), Specialist Knowledge and Ability (19), Teamwork and Collaboration (20).

KEY 10

Interpersonal Awareness and Diplomacy

Interpersonal Awareness and Diplomacy

People who are interpersonally aware demonstrate respect and consideration for different views and perspectives. They relate well to diverse groups and can operate in a variety of cultural settings. Great at investing time and energy to establish rapport and build common ground, these tactful individuals leave people with the impression that they are valued. They use their self-awareness to better understand those around them and adapt their behaviour accordingly. Capable of empathising with the feelings and emotions of others, they will foster harmonious relationships and minimise any potential for conflict. They are diplomatic in their approach and always strive to maintain impartiality.

Ideas for personal development

> *The shoe that fits one person pinches another; there is no recipe for living that suits all cases.*
>
> **Carl Jung**

Tools

- Strengthen your own levels of emotional awareness. Learn to identify, label and deal with complex emotions using Dr Robert Plutchik's 'wheel of emotions'.[137] This visual colour wheel tool can be used to understand the relationship between eight primary emotions and other related states to provide a greater insight into the combinations of emotions and their implications.

Assess how emotionally intelligent you are. Use Simon Baron-Cohen's 'Reading the Mind in the Eyes' test to investigate how effective you are likely to be at picking up on the unspoken feelings and emotions of others. Use the results of this well-researched test as a potential indicator as to your ability to empathise with others in social situations.[138]

Techniques

Demonstrate you care about others. Make an extra effort to say thank you and always be sincere with your gratitude. Be humble, polite and courteous to break down any defensiveness. Remember names and respect the views of others. Build rapport by promoting areas of common ground.

Openly express what you think and feel, but remember that while diplomacy has been described as the art of letting someone have your way, tact is the art of making a point without creating an enemy.

Retain an even tone of voice and choose your words carefully. 'Always', 'never', 'should', 'ought' and 'must' are all loaded words.

Get to know people. Master small talk. Learn about the demands and challenges faced by others. Be a team player and offer support to others who need assistance. Make an effort to talk to people outside your immediate workgroup during company events.

Keep an open mind. Test any assumptions you hold by asking questions and then paraphrasing what you have heard. Enter every discussion willing to listen intently to the other person.

Suspend your ego and the need to be right. Avoid correcting people or introducing anything which could be perceived as one-upmanship. You don't need to tell them your story – just encourage them to share theirs.

Be patient. Wait for others to have their say or provide their opinions before offering your own. When presenting negative information, try to highlight at least one positive aspect.

Inspiration

✤ Follow the brilliant and straightforward advice by Celeste Headlee in her TED Talk 'Ten Ways to Have a Better Conversation'.[139]

 Ideas for delivering results

> *They may forget what you said – but they will never forget how you made them feel.*
>
> **Carl W. Buehner**

Tool

▣ Research David Merrill and Roger Reid's social styles model.[140] This simple tool focuses on behaviour rather than psychological preferences, and can be used to support an understanding of how people sometimes interact based on their levels of assertiveness and responsiveness. It was originally devised as a tool to predict success in management careers.

Techniques

▲ Learn to flex your communication style and modify your approach to meet the needs of those around you.

▲ Adopt relationship building non-verbal behaviour. The impact of a simple smile can be accentuated by adding a slight head tilt to show you are comfortable with the person and trust them. Another non-verbal technique is to try to maintain a slightly lowered chin angle (high chins can make people feel you are looking down at them).

▲ Diplomatic communicators excel at listening, considering options and being open. They consciously evaluate first, then choose if, how and when to make their contribution.

▲ Tell the truth in a way that considers other people's feelings and responses, ensuring that your rights and the rights of the other party are respected. Use indirect language when appropriate to avoid appearing dogmatic and inflexible: 'It looks like …', 'What I am hearing is …', 'My understanding is …'

▲ Build rapport by asking for help. When a request is small, we naturally feel a connection with those who ask for assistance. Similarly, an occasional small gift can promote a desire to reciprocate.

▲ Avoid getting involved with the negativity gang at work – distance yourself from the jaundiced and cynical colleagues who dwell on the past. Try not to talk behind people's backs or get pulled into petty gossiping.

▲ Exercise self-regulation. Practise waiting a few minutes, a few hours or a few days before responding to an emotionally charged situation.

▲ Relax your posture, voice and body language. Try to appear at ease, even if you don't feel it. Speak slowly and deliberately and try to avoid lots of gesticulating or fast arm movements, which can be distracting.

▲ Focus on the facts. Master the skill of graceful confrontation by removing any underlying layers of emotion to ease unwanted stress. Be honest but tactful, and maintain composure if tempers flare.

▲ Solve issues by working through the recognised organisational structure. Attempt to talk with your line manager first before escalating any problem upwards. Don't go over people's heads. If tension exists, try resolving it first.

▲ Actively attempt to always deal with the problem, not the person. Be aware that we tend to judge ourselves by our intentions and others by their actions. The two are rarely the same, so always endeavour to understand the intentions of others before trying to resolve different points of view.

▲ Listen, rephrase and repeat. According to Marshall Rosenberg, studies of industrial relations negotiations demonstrate that the time required to reach conflict resolution is cut in half when each negotiator agrees to repeat what the previous speaker has said before they begin to respond.[141]

▲ Praise in public, criticise in private. Solve problems behind closed doors to maintain morale and prevent issues from impacting on others. Try not to take personally any negative feedback you may receive.

▲ Ask a trusted friend for unguarded feedback on how you come across under duress. Proactively seek feedback from peers and colleagues on your work approaches as often as possible.

▲ Be consistent and always honour your commitments.

Inspiration

✛ Learn how to be more aware of your emotions at work. Discover techniques to respond to situations at work in a calm and composed way by reading *Why Buddhism is True* by Robert Wright.[142] Recognise people who provide you with an increased sense of vitality and aliveness when you are in their presence. Be aware of the impact these individuals bring and try to spend more time with them.

✛ Wise men speak because they have something to say, fools because they have to say something. Consider Diplomat Charles-Maurice de Talleyrand-Perigord, who apparently said 'Surtout, pas trop de zele' – which translates as 'Above all, not too much zeal.'

✛ Pore over *Emotional Intelligence* by Daniel Goleman,[143] then devour *Never Eat Alone* by Keith Ferrazzi and Tahl Raz.[144]

✛ Watch Dan Shapiro's video 'How to Resolve Any Argument'.[145] Discover effective ways to bring two opposing sides together and resolve any conflict.

Ideas for long-term gain

> *Our emotional intelligence determines our potential for learning the practical skills that are based on its five elements: self-awareness, motivation, self-regulation, empathy, and adeptness in relationships.*
>
> **Daniel Goleman**

Tools

- Try completing a Johari Window exercise to help you understand your relationships with others.[146] Remove your work mask and reveal any blind spots not known to yourself or those around you.

- Complete a 360 degree profile and encourage at least eight of your colleagues to participate in the process and provide feedback on your approach. Ideally use a tool which focuses on emotional intelligence, such as the Hay Group's Emotional and Social Competency Inventory (ESCI).[147]

- Schedule plenty of physical breaks away from work and remember to take mental breaks too. Download a free app such as Headspace from the App Store or Google Play to help you relax, recharge and return to work ready to face the challenges of the day.

Techniques

- Embrace difference including cultural variations. Leverage variation to assemble great teams and assign different talents to specific situations.

- Share credit for things – even if you did most of the work. One of the fastest ways to build effective relations with others is to be generous during moments of high visibility. When others feel that you respect them, they will be more likely to respect you in return.

- Encourage more open and unguarded conversations. If a relationship is already established, try out this simple question, 'What is it that you really want?', and then really listen to people's responses. It's a question which is 100 per cent focused on the other person and can be quite revealing.

- Extend your emotional vocabulary. Be skilled at articulating how you feel and confident in expressing what you observe around you. If possible, work with a personal coach to improve your emotional quotient (EQ) levels.

- Become the go-to person for mediating issues and resolving conflict. Be a problem solver and someone who explores solutions. Build integrity by being calm, fair and even handed, and committed to finding the best outcome for all parties.

Inspiration

- Look into Richard Thaler and Cass Sunstein's nudge theory. Master the art of being friendly with a purpose by reading their book *Nudge: Improving Decisions About Health, Wealth and Happiness*.[148]

- Exercise learned optimism. While pessimists tend to make global, permanent and internally attributed reasons for things that happen, optimists pull people towards them by making specific, temporary and externally attributed reasons when confronted by setbacks. To find out how to switch this habit, read *Learned Optimism* by Martin Seligman.[149]

Interpersonal Awareness and Diplomacy

Related work skills

Ability to Influence (1), Constructive Communication (4), Enthusiasm for Customer Service (8), Focus on Developing Others (9), Intuitive Thought (11), Resilience and Emotional Control (17).

Intuitive Thought

Intuitive Thought

People who are highly intuitive develop a reputation for providing effective judgement. In most cases, they will demonstrate understanding and insight which occurs outside of the traditional thinking process. They are comfortable following their own instincts and are likely to excel at noticing patterns and recognising connections. They trust their own convictions that they understand what information is important, without instruction. These individuals have a capacity for detecting and interpreting meaning from indirect, interpersonal signals such as non-verbal communication, body language, inference and inflection.

Ideas for personal development

> *You must train your intuition – you must trust the small voice inside you which tells you exactly what to say, what to decide.*
>
> **Ingrid Bergman**

Tool

- Flip a coin. If you're unsure about what to do and have two different options to choose from, assign an option to each side of a coin and then flip it in the air as high as you can. Just as you release the coin, you may recognise your internal voice telling you on which side you would prefer it to land. You may also sense a slight feeling of disappointment if it lands on the side you weren't really hoping for.

Techniques

▲ Release your resistance. Our rational mind usually distrusts intuitive thinking because it overestimates the risks involved with non-logical decision making, yet it could be ignoring flashes of inspiration which might move your thinking forwards.

▲ Learn to differentiate between thinking and feeling. Consciously stop to consider what is driving your sensations at certain moments of the day. Studies show when you ignore your intuition, the quality of your decision making drops.[150]

▲ Relax and practise being still. Signals from your subconscious tend to be very quiet, so you need to be silent to be able to pick these up clearly.

▲ Consciously practise switching attention between each of your five senses. Focus on using each in turn at different moments during the day. Using this exercise can raise your awareness of the messages you receive through your sixth sense.

▲ Engage in repetitive movements. This is a proven method of occupying your rational mind, without overtaxing it.[151] Mozart meticulously counted out the sixty beans for his morning coffee every single day. Chop vegetables, paint the fence, go for a run. These activities can calm cognitive processes and help you to access your intuitive mind.

▲ Listen to your physiology and develop somatic awareness. If you have an uncomfortable feeling about a particular work decision, recognise this and pay attention to it.

▲ Read more about your field of study. While much of our intuition is shaped by our ability to recall similar situations, there is no substitute for breadth of experience. Many successful entrepreneurs who rely on their instincts develop new ways of looking at things by dedicating time to read prolifically.

▲ Get away. Spend time away from the problem, remove your watch, ignore the clock and leave technology in the office. Escape your daily routines, clear your schedule and slow down.

Inspiration

✛ Live in the now. Savour the present. If you are consumed by anxieties about the future, you will not be able to use your intuition. Similarly, if much of your time is spent ruminating on what has happened in the past then this will take up too much mental capacity to allow your intuitive hunches to rise to the fore. Studies confirm that being in a positive mood boosts your ability to make intuitive judgements.[152]

⚙ Ideas for delivering results

A woman's guess is much more accurate than a man's certainty.

Rudyard Kipling

Tool

▦ Complete a moral compass exercise. There are times when your conscious mind may steer you away from the things you value the most; however, your unconscious, intuitive self is likely to remain true to your values.

Techniques

▲ Become a reader of patterns. Highly intuitive people are adept at recognising patterns in situations and events. They pick them up easily and are quick to make associations.

- Test your hunches and start to act on them. If you ever experience a feeling about a particular project or situation, recognise this sensation. Make a note of how and when it arose and then revisit your observations sometime after the event. Repeat this process whenever you feel the same sensation and try to identify any patterns which are emerging.

- Pick up and interpret meaning from indirect and interpersonal signals such as inference, inflection and non-verbal clues.

- Apply sense making methods. Consciously try to size up situations more quickly and with less forced effort. Deliberately extend your desire to capture the essence of a problem and spot any anomalies at an earlier stage.

- If you are hesitant about relying on your unconscious, non-analytical brain, test it out during non-critical negotiations to save time and reflect on the outcome you achieved. Alternatively, try using a traffic light system to increase your awareness of both logical and non-rational thoughts. When making a decision, if both your intuition and analysis say no, then this is a red light. If both say yes, this is a green light. If one or the other says no, then this is amber, so you may need to proceed with caution.

- Volunteer to contribute to projects and tasks which will provide opportunities to validate your self-belief and build your self-confidence. Assured people have strong personal resolve. They trust their instincts and as a result generate trust in others, which further develops belief in their own abilities.

- Avoid reliance on too many measurements and metrics, both of which reduce the potential for intuitive thinking.

- Develop the ability to be more comfortable with ambiguity and uncertainty. Evidence suggests that highly intuitive individuals may be perceived as more risk orientated, when in fact they are simply more adept at dealing with the unknown.[153]

- Be known as an ambassador for following your own judgements and being comfortable questioning established systems as required. Actively support work processes which encourage the demonstration of effective and timely judgements by all your peers.

- ▲ Be an expert. Remember that those with a higher degree of expertise in a subject consistently perform better in tests requiring intuition when compared to novices. Fighter pilots regularly experience a sense of precognition.[154]

- ▲ Become an effective role model by being especially receptive to new ideas and alternative suggestions. Encourage your team to redefine intuition as a way of translating evidence into action – as a natural and direct outcome of previous learnings.

- ▲ Hone team members' intuition by supporting their professional development, extending their breadth of experience and providing sneak-peeks into future projects you will be working on. Make sure they understand pressing priorities.

- ▲ Gravitate towards upbeat innovators who value the acquisition of knowledge and are drawn to future possibilities. Spend more time with people who are excited about challenges and moving things forward. Typically, these tenacious individuals excel at improvising and developing creative solutions.

Inspiration

- ✛ Practise creativity techniques in your spare time. Instead of using lists, why not draw, use mind maps or rich pictures to represent ideas and concepts. If you don't feel comfortable with your artistic abilities, watch Graham Shaw's TEDx Talk 'Why People Believe They Can't Draw'.[155] Try out other non-linear activities such as playing games and doing mental puzzles.

- ✛ Go Greek. Thumb slowly through an old copy of *Zorba the Greek* by Nikos Kazantzakis and celebrate the joys of a more instinctive approach.[156] Challenge yourself to step outside of your rational brain and acknowledge the limitations of over-thinking.

- ✛ Spread the word. If colleagues remain unconvinced about 'informed hunches', quote them a bit of Einstein, who reportedly said, 'The only valuable thing is intuition', and applied this belief when developing the now proven theory of relativity. Steve Jobs, Bill Gates and Richard Branson have all shared a similar conviction.

- Practise acting without thinking. Pick up a copy of Malcolm Gladwell's book *Blink* and learn how decisions made quickly can be every bit as good as decisions made slowly and deliberately.[157]

- Watch the TEDx Talk by Dr Ivan Joseph entitled 'The Skill of Self-Confidence' and hear about the importance of trusting yourself.[158]

- Create a great new business idea after reading *Hunch: Turn Your Everyday Insights Into the Next Big Thing* by Bernadette Jiwa.[159]

Ideas for long-term gain

> *... you can't connect the dots looking forward; you can only connect them looking backward. So you have to trust that the dots will somehow connect in your future. You have to trust in something – your gut, destiny, life, karma, whatever. This approach has never let me down, and it has made all the difference in my life.*
>
> **Steve Jobs**

Tool

- Increase your intuitive decision making skills by putting yourself through a programme of mental conditioning using cognitive strategies including decision games, decision requirement tables and pre-mortems to expand your pattern recognition abilities.

Techniques

▲ Awake your unconscious by fostering the right learning environment. Intuitive decisions improve with practice. Generate more opportunities by supporting a culture which tolerates mistakes and encourages others to have confidence in their experience and instincts.

▲ Use situational assessments and real-life case studies from your own sector. Investigating the outcomes of previous similar situations can improve decision making and reveal patterns for your intuition to follow.

▲ Win over sceptics by presenting a balanced approach to risk analysis. Remember to recognise potential threats to success even in situations where there is little precedent set or previous examples from which to learn.

▲ Know when to apply intuitive thought. Eugene Sadler-Smith suggests that intuitive thought processes are beneficial for creative endeavours and even more helpful when you are tasked with ethical decision making.[160]

▲ Coach others to develop their intuitive instincts. Encourage them to lay out events on a timeline and identify when similar events occurred. Probe for specific incidents and examples. Ask about the trends and patterns they can see. Expand their thinking by posing lots of 'what if?' questions.

▲ Promote clear personal values and beliefs to provide a consistent platform for yourself when dealing with less familiar circumstances.

Inspiration

➕ Research Ap Dijksterhuis and Zeger van Olden and discover simple ways to apply your unconscious mind when tasked with making more complex choices.[161]

- Recognise what works for you and follow your own path. Warren Buffett has had greater success as an investor than any other individual in history, yet he doesn't follow the investment trends or the advice of other investors. He sticks to businesses he understands well and only acts on an investment if he feels it is right to do so.[162]

- Follow the advice of Gary Klein in his book *The Power of Intuition*.[163] Apply his three-tier programme to build advanced intuition, make tough choices and size up situations quickly.

 ## Related work skills

Creativity and Innovation (5), Interpersonal Awareness and Diplomacy (10), Ownership of Self-Development (13), Positive Decisions (15), Resilience and Emotional Control (17).

KEY 12

Motivation to Succeed

Motivation to Succeed

People who are motivated to succeed encourage themselves and others to deliver optimum results through repeated effort. They are challenged by demanding targets and work hard to achieve them. These individuals have a clear and compelling reason for acting in a particular way and push themselves to do things better. They approach tasks with a positive mindset and typically they will demonstrate high levels of personal drive. Great at embracing continual improvement in both their professional and personal life, they are both persistent and tenacious in seeing work through to its conclusion.

 ## Ideas for personal development

> *Nobody succeeds beyond his or her wildest expectations unless he or she begins with some wild expectations.*
>
> **Ralph Charell**

Tools

- Build personal motivation through use of commitment contracts.[164] If you are concerned that you may struggle to see something through, try establishing a contract with a peer or respected friend, where you agree some consequence for not completing your task by a date which is agreed in advance. This could involve donating some cash to charity if you do not deliver on time.

Forget Abraham Maslow. He presented a very accessible little model of motivation, supported by a charming little pyramid, but ultimately his methodology lacked scientific rigour. While his work on basic human needs provides a useful starting place, many critics believe his theory takes little account of the complexity of individual motivations in the modern workplace.[165]

Techniques

Push beyond your comfort zones. Remember, setting challenging goals which are both tasking and achievable will always result in higher performance than no goal at all. Chart your progress to monitor your development and retain your focus.

Motivation comes from the Latin word *movere* and means reason for action. Without a motive there is no reason. Begin to explore your rationale for doing something. Ask yourself three simple questions to increase personal drive: (1) What is most important to me? (2) What is the first small step I can take? (3) When do I want to do it by?

Be prepared to change your work routines and practices to achieve the results you want. Create informal milestones along the way and celebrate their achievement to prevent complacency.

Get chemical. If you aren't feeling especially motivated, select a tiny, rather easy part of the task to begin with. Dopamine is produced every time you achieve something, no matter how small this is.

Approach all your tasks with a resilient mindset. Take pride in your achievements and repeat your efforts to achieve optimum results. You become what you think about the most. Ask yourself what you think about the most. Write down what it is you want to become and where you would like to be. Read this every night before going to sleep.

Spot your triggers. We all have them. Some triggers energise us, fire us up and make us more focused. Other people and situations can sap our strength and drain our resources. Reflect on both and begin to recognise when each of these occur.

Inspiration

✛ It is okay to associate activity and action with achievement and success, but don't forget to enjoy at least part of what you do. If you don't, you won't be able to maintain your motivation for very long. Find out how to be micro-ambitious by watching Tim Minchin's speech on YouTube entitled 'Don't Die Unhappy – Learn These 9 Life Lessons'.[166]

✛ Stop completing things! Keep yourself productive all day by pausing when the going is good, rather than trying to get everything completed by lunchtime. According to Ernest Hemingway, if you make yourself stop, put everything down and walk away, then you can't wait to get back to it, because you have built up an expectation for what is required next. Stopping in this way will keep you interested and reduce any psychological barriers to returning to the task. Investigate the Zeigarnik effect to find out more.[167]

⚙ Ideas for delivering results

> *… we have three innate psychological needs – competence, autonomy, and relatedness. When those needs are satisfied, we're motivated, productive, and happy.*
>
> **Daniel Pink**

Tools

▪ Adopt a planned and purposeful approach to task resolution. Write down your goals, give yourself a deadline and reward progress. Google Chrome extensions like Prioritab can help to keep your short-term daily, weekly and monthly goals in sight.

To appreciate a few of the more common generic drivers in the workplace, ask your colleagues to complete a questionnaire based on Herzberg's two-factor theory of motivation.[168] Although this is an old model, its results have been replicated every decade since its inception.

Techniques

Forget 'positive thinking' and instead try out 'mental contrasting' to increase goal attainment.[169] After you identify a stretching goal for yourself, reflect on what may be holding you back from achieving it. Imagine all the obstacles in vivid detail and then develop a plan to overcome them all.

Create detailed plans to achieve your goals. Motivate yourself by breaking goals into sub-goals and then create a step-by-step process to achieve each of these. Research suggests that people are far more likely to achieve their goals when they focus on process rather than outcome.[170]

Build anticipation for big goals. Ignore conventional thinking and don't 'do it now'. Instead, hold back from launching straight into a big goal. Defer the launch, publicise your intentions and tell everyone about it first. Make it an event to look forward to and get everyone on board first with a countdown to the launch day.

Encourage your team to speak positively about their workgroup and organisation. Develop their sense of connectivity to it and help each person to strive to do more by going beyond what is expected.

Resist the temptation to associate motivation with being happy or satisfied. Mountain climbers experience very few moments of joy and their days are usually filled with challenging circumstances.

Get involved. Socialising in and out of the workplace accelerates interpersonal commitment by binding people together.

Motivation to Succeed

- Consider that well-managed team-building events can positively impact on morale, motivation and performance levels, especially if they focus on building trust, open communication and collaborative effort.

- Remove the office clock. Apply casino mentality and focus on the task, not the time. Research demonstrates that reminding people of how much time has passed impedes performance on many non-standardised tasks.[171] Become internally referenced, not externally referenced.

- Get equitable. Acknowledge that personal motivation in the West is strongly influenced by perceived market norms. Motivation extends beyond simply what you put into a job versus what you get out of it. Levels of personal drive are also shaped by individual perceptions of what others, who are similar to ourselves, are receiving. Look up J. Stacy Adams' equity theory to find out how this works.[172]

- Don't believe the hype. Resist fantasising about a desired future state or relying on visualisation techniques to improve your chances of success. While these methods were popular in the 1990s, new research illustrates that individuals who invest in visualisation methods to help them achieve their goals consistently fare less well than those who do not.[173] It is suggested that individuals who regularly visualise future images of success may be less prepared for setbacks along the way.

- Surround yourself with the right people. Being focused and inspired is contagious. Catch it and pass it on. If you are ever feeling in a rut or less than appreciated, create a file full of all your positive feedback from others and revisit these comments on a regular basis.

- Manage motivation by mouth. Catecholamines are important for relieving stress, boosting mental energy and sustaining motivation. Keep your own levels high by eating the right foods. Catecholamines are constructed from the amino acid L-tyrosine, which is commonly found in foods such as salmon, soya beans, turkey, seaweed and chicken.

Inspiration

✦ Read *The Miracle Morning: The 6 Habits That Will Transform Your Life Before 8am* by Hal Elrod and discover how to wake up every day with more energy, motivation and focus.[174]

✦ Buy some coloured ribbon. When motivating others, Napoleon Bonaparte is believed to have said, 'I could conquer the world if only I had enough ribbon.' He had apparently discovered that while his soldiers were prepared to fight for money, they were willing to die for medals and ribbons. Explore ways to provide a greater sense of recognition. Take the time to write personal, handwritten letters of thanks.

✦ Search out Hugo Kehr's TEDx Talk entitled 'Motivate Yourself with Visions, Goals and Willpower' to discover some deceptively simple tactics to reach maximum motivation, avoid distraction and achieve your goals.[175]

✦ Swim the Hellespont, or at the very least read the article by Charles Foster on swimming the Hellespont and consider what motivational forces demonstrated in it can be applied in the workplace.[176]

✦ Get yourself a copy of Daniel Pink's book *Drive*,[177] and then watch his TED Talk entitled 'The Puzzle of Motivation'.[178]

✦ Accept that it is easier to inspire someone than it is to motivate them. Flick through *The Influential Mind: What the Brain Reveals About Our Power to Change Others* by Tali Sharot.[179] Discover why it is so difficult to modify the attitudes and actions of others, and pick up some simple methods to inspire people through positive reinforcement.

Motivation to Succeed

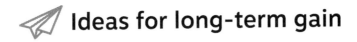# Ideas for long-term gain

> *Building a boat isn't about weaving canvas, forging nails, or reading the sky. It's about giving a shared taste for the sea.*
>
> **Antoine de Saint-Exupéry**

Tool

▪ Request all your team complete the Gallup Q12 Employee Engagement survey (or similar questionnaire), collectively discuss the results and then build an action plan for any areas of common dissatisfaction.

Techniques

▲ Consider the possibility that we are all 100 per cent motivated – all of the time. The only question is to identify what each person is motivated by at a particular time. Some people arrive at work motivated to get through the day with the minimum fuss and leave by 16.59.

▲ Beware of applying the wrong incentives at the wrong time. While financial incentives may work in the short term for straightforward operational tasks, the same incentives have also been found to block more inventive thinking and can lessen our ability to perform under pressure.[180]

▲ Ditch the rhetoric. Remove motivational posters from around the office. For 90 per cent of people, being told 'Anything is possible' has the opposite effect to the one intended. Instead, communicate a clear story of the big picture and let all your team know how they will personally contribute to it.

▲ To increase personal energy and commitment, think about how the strength of electric current is measured and apply AMP to your work situation. Move your focus from extrinsic motivators (such as incentives and bonuses) to intrinsic motivators (getting people to do something because they want to do it). Look for opportunities to extend levels of personal Autonomy, Mastery and Purpose to motivate those around you. These three principles appeal to our innate desire to direct our own lives, become more skilful at something and be part of a bigger picture.

▲ Remind yourself that very few people wash a rented car. If you want to build motivation, provide people with a sense of ownership. People will struggle to push harder without a degree of personal responsibility for what happens.

▲ Be mindful that the single biggest influencer of levels of workplace engagement is the relationship an employee has with their line manager. Exit interviews reveal that more people leave their manager than leave their work content,[181] so invest in making this relationship a good one.

Inspiration

+ Acknowledge the work of Dan Ariely, who demonstrated that the less appreciated we feel at work, the more money we want; also, the harder a project is, the prouder we feel about it on completion. Read his book *Payoff* to discover the importance of how we value our work.[182]

+ Peruse *The Extra Mile* by David Macleod and Chris Brady and apply the practical ideas to your own workgroup. Apply their acid test statement to yourself and others: '(1) I believe that rewards are fairly distributed. (2) I feel respected and listened to. (3) I am improving my skills. (4) I believe my organisation has a sincere interest in supporting me.'[183]

+ Build belief. Google 'Vroom's expectancy theory' and apply it to evaluate your most pressing work challenge. Victor Vroom believed that motivation was a personal construct, created by a mixture of our desire to do something multiplied by our belief that the outcome is possible. Essentially, if you aren't motivated then either you aren't interested in achieving it or you don't feel it is likely to be achieved.

Related work skills

Commitment to Change and Adaptation (3), Ownership of Self-Development (13), People Management and Leadership Potential (14), Resilience and Emotional Control (17), Results through Action (18), Specialist Knowledge and Ability (19).

Motivation to Succeed

Ownership of Self-Development

Ownership of Self-Development

People who are committed to personal development at work are attracted towards possibilities for professional growth. They continually stretch themselves and demonstrate an appetite for further learning. By accepting responsibility for their self-improvement, they exhibit a willingness to learn and extend their existing abilities and experiences. They excel at keeping up to date with emerging approaches and share their knowledge freely. These individuals regularly review their performance and reflect on progress made, to identify new learning goals. They learn from both their successes and failures and actively seek feedback from others to change and improve.

Ideas for personal development

> *I think of my career as a jungle gym, not a ladder: jumping from rung to rung, side to side, up and down, learning new things, pursuing new experiences, and focusing as much on the journey as the destination.*
>
> **Lori Goler**

Tools

- Use to-do lists to keep on top of small tasks. If you sit at a PC for most of the day, try out one of the many free personal organisation tools available online, such as Stickies, 7 Sticky Notes or the free version of Notezilla. Bear in mind that it may also be helpful to create not-to-do lists – highlighting things you wish to stop doing. These can be simpler to achieve and may make it easier for you to focus on the tasks you do want to achieve.

- Be open to new ideas. Visit openculture.com and explore their comprehensive selection of free learning resources, including courses, lectures, language lessons and e-books. If you enjoy learning by watching videos, visit curiosity.com for thousands of online personal growth videos. Alternatively, head over to gohighbrow.com to receive a personalised five-minute course in your inbox every day of the year.

- Begin a journal. Personal reflection is a great way to develop self-awareness and capture all your important observations. Keep an ideas file containing unusual personal development suggestions and innovative ideas. Review your entries at the end of every week. It doesn't matter whether you use a tatty old notebook, a leather binder or one of the new online sites such as 750words.com – where you can write whatever comes to mind and then receive feedback on your emotions and thoughts.

Techniques

- Identify your strengths and development areas. Get feedback from others. Differentiate between things you would like to start doing, continue doing, stop doing and do differently. Select an area to work on and be accountable for it.

- Read more. Commit to your personal development and set a target to read at least one personal development article every day.

- Narrow your focus. Don't try to 'fix' everything. Concentrate your energies on defined areas to prevent your efforts being diffused by lots of conflicting priorities.

- Be incurably curious. Ask lots of questions. Keep your brain power honed. Learn a language to keep your synapses firing.[184] Alternatively, play a strategy game like chess to extend your analytical skills.[185]

Inspiration

+ Habit, habit, habit. Routinely wake up thirty minutes earlier and use this extra time to set the tone for the day ahead. Back in the nineteenth century, social reformer Henry Ward Beecher stated, 'The first hour of the morning is the rudder of the day.' The ability to find pockets of extra time to invest in ourselves and stop feeling so rushed is even more relevant in today's hectic world. Successful development coaches, including Robin Sharma, advocate waking up between 5am and 6am each day to help improve productivity and quality of life.

+ Keep yourself vital by referring to the powerful observation, believed to have been made by Leonardo da Vinci, that 'learning never exhausts the mind'.

+ Get an earful. Virtually everyone has heard of TED Talks, but if you prefer to learn while on the go, try tuning in to the TED Radio Hour show at npr.org, which delivers thought-provoking podcasts by some remarkable people. Alternatively, listen to the 'Tell Me Something I Don't Know' podcasts by Stephen J. Dubner on iTunes – great for reminding yourself that you don't know what you don't know.

⚙ Ideas for delivering results

13

> *Every person I work with knows something better than me. My job is to listen long enough to find it and use it.*
>
> **Jack Nichols**

Tools

▪ Open a WordPress account and create a blog about your personal learning journey. Not only will it help you to organise your thinking, it will also encourage others to engage and contribute to your ongoing development.

- Become your team's local advocate for continuous professional development. Actively pursue all relevant learning and development opportunities available to you. Get an Ivy League education for free and complete your studies at your own pace using Open Yale Courses and Stanford Online, both of which are packed with hundreds of video courses on everything from finance to psychology.

- Know yourself and recognise any blind spots. Search the web or look at the Kindle version of Julie Hay's *Working It Out At Work* for a version of a working styles inventory.[186] This questionnaire will help you to identify which of the working style drivers you are most likely to adopt. Consider the consequences of these preferences and how they may influence your responses during any stressful situations.

- Use the Feynman Technique to create clear, simple explanations of important information.[187] Applying this four-step method will also help you to learn anything faster than you ever could without it.

- Supplement your formal development offerings with some self-directed learning opportunities. To access free online learning modules through massive open online courses (MOOCs), visit alison.com and coursera.com. Focus on one or two programmes at a time to avoid overloading yourself, and be aware that certain knowledge-based learning programmes may involve less deep processing of the materials presented.

Techniques

▲ Get a mentor.

▲ Be honest and ask yourself, 'Just how open am I really to asking for help from others?' Drop the defensiveness when receiving any constructive feedback. Signal your receptivity by using statements such as, 'You are right – this is something I recognise and am currently working on.'

▲ For any learning undertaken, try to apply the 2R + 2A formula. Recognise what you have picked up, Relate it to something you already know, Assimilate what you have covered and then Apply the learning.

- Make a point of deliberately learning from your successes. We are often told to build on our failures, but you should also remember to consider what went right, what you can apply again and what would make it even more successful next time.

- Choose who you surround yourself with. Entrepreneur Jim Rohn famously observed that we are all the average of the five people with whom we spend the most time. This is based on the law of averages, which states that the result of any given situation will be the average of all outcomes. Who you spend your time with may therefore impact on who you become.

- Try a role swap, a secondment or elect to spend time in a different department. Build new connections and extend your knowledge of how other teams operate.

- Share your learning and save time by picking up on the learning experiences of others, rather than having to test everything yourself. As Benjamin Franklin allegedly once said: 'There are two ways to acquire wisdom; you can either buy it or borrow it. By buying it, you pay full price in terms of time and cost to learn the lessons you need to learn. By borrowing it, you go to those men and women who have already paid the price to learn the lessons and get their wisdom from them.'

- Remember much more of what you learn by using spaced repetition. Follow the design of the latest learning-based software and improve personal retention levels by repeating any learned material over increasingly spaced intervals. This technique requires greater effort, which has been proven to enhance your ability to recall information at a later date.[188]

- Provide your colleagues with plenty of opportunities to apply any training undertaken to help build their confidence, assist with the retention of learning and generate a return on investment.

- Construct a brilliant curriculum vitae or résumé, even if you aren't looking to change roles. Focus on professional results, not your work responsibilities, and keep it accessible. Update this document on a regular basis and create a range of different personal statements which can be interchanged to appeal to different potential markets.

13

Inspiration

+ Find your inner gladiator. Read *The Art of Learning* by international chess prodigy and Tai Chi champion Josh Waitzkin.[189] Pick up proven ways to learn more quickly and move from beginner to expert in any discipline. Discover how some of the most sophisticated learning techniques have their foundations in the simplest of principles.

+ Eliminate any non-essential activities to provide more time to focus on what is important for your development. Read *The 4-Hour Work Week* by Timothy Ferriss.[190] His TED Talk entitled 'Smash Fear, Learn Anything' is also worth watching.[191]

+ Be growth orientated rather than task orientated. Gain insight in terms of how to achieve this by watching Suzanne Eder's TEDx Talk entitled 'The Dark Side of Self Improvement'.[192]

+ Take a look at how one Google employee goes about setting and achieving his personal development goals in the video 'Try Something New for 30 days' by Matt Cutts.[193]

+ Find ways to reduce your playing field. If you are looking to acquire a new skill – improve at sports, learn a musical instrument or excel at a new work application – read about the Futsal principle in Daniel Coyle's book *The Talent Code*.[194] You will discover unexpected ways to improve performance, such as how Brazil came to dominate world soccer by deliberately shrinking their playing field and using a heavier ball in order to develop superior ball control.

Ideas for long-term gain

Tool

■ Set yourself GBOGs. Great Big Outrageous Goals shouldn't work, but they do. They stretch you out of the ordinary and are so ambitious they can resonate with you and others. They offer the power to elevate us beyond what we thought was possible. At the age of sixteen, Winston Churchill shared his GBOG and was quoted as saying, 'I tell you I shall be in command of the defences of London … in the high position I shall occupy, it will fall to me to save the Capital and save the Empire.'[195]

Techniques

▲ Help a local superstar. High performers are left to fend for themselves and rarely receive dedicated assistance because it is often assumed they are capable. This may feel counterintuitive, but helping highly proficient people will not only make them grateful and strengthen rapport, but you may also pick up a thing or two about their approach.

▲ Prioritise the development of inter-organisational transferable skills, including operational agility, change orientation, creative thinking and collaborative effort.

▲ Apply accelerated learning techniques. Use short bursts of high input learning followed by frequent rests throughout the day, then teach someone else what you've covered in order to consolidate your understanding of the subject.

- Meet more people. Connect with the top people and respected authorities in your field of interest. Link up with them on social media, send them your best idea or offer them some support on one of their important projects.

- Be generous in your recognition and celebration of others who have achieved personal milestones in their own development plans.

- Get entrepreneurial and launch a small business venture. However modest an enterprise this may be, it will expose you to valuable lessons in management, marketing, finance and customer relations. If you are considering launching your own business, listen to practical advice on how to start a new venture at thepodcasthost.com. For advice on how some of the world's most successful entrepreneurs went on to make their business a success, try out the 'How I Built This' podcasts by Guy Raz.

- Create a PLN (Personal Learning Network) with a handful of peers who share your passion for learning. Consider using a facilitator to manage any physical meetings and challenge your thinking.

Inspiration

+ Develop your inner Dilbert. Read *How to Fail at Almost Everything and Still Win Big* by Dilbert comic strip creator Scott Adams.[196] Uncover unusual and effective ways to embrace failure while building a successful career.

+ Investigate opportunities to learn through local community groups and voluntary organisations to provide an effective development platform for you and others. Listen to podcasts by philanthropists like Tuan Nguyen to get inspired.

 # Related work skills

Focus on Developing Others (9), Intuitive Thought (11), Motivation to Succeed (12), Resilience and Emotional Control (17), Results through Action (18), Specialist Knowledge and Ability (19).

People Management and Leadership Potential

People Management and Leadership Potential

Individuals with management and leadership capability excel at delivering results through engaging other people. They take charge when required and are able to direct others towards the achievement of defined goals through the use of inspiration and encouragement. They share responsibility and delegate widely. Great at communicating expected outcomes, they are able to help others to believe that success is possible by providing them with permission to act and by acknowledging contributions. These individuals ensure that the necessary tasks are handled by the most suitable team members. They are capable of translating complex strategy into meaningful activity. By operating with transparency and modelling appropriate behaviour, they project credibility, supporting and challenging those around them to be more accountable for performance improvements.

 ## Ideas for personal development

> *Leadership is the art of giving people a platform for spreading ideas that work.*
>
> **Seth Godin**

Tool

- Apply the Stephen Covey formula for success in your role: vision, passion and discipline, governed by conscience. Ghandi possessed all four, while Hitler had only three.[197]

Techniques

▲ Understand the organisation you work in. Know what is happening to enable you to make informed decisions. Be clear about your operational priorities and share them with all your team. A recent poll by Harris Interactive revealed that very few people are able to name their most important work goals.[198]

▲ Taking on more responsibility means that relationships will change and you will need to be transparent about this. Set clear ground rules from the outset and have an honest conversation with people about expectations.

▲ Be visible. Stay in the trenches. People will follow your lead if they can see you are prepared to undertake any job to move things forward. 'Walking the walk' has been shown to be one of the most effective employee engagement strategies a leader can employ.[199]

▲ Set the tone – deal with the people issues first. Manage yourself in a way which makes it easy for others to want to follow. Talk like a human. Model the behaviours you want others to repeat and always be consistent.

▲ Identify a management style which works for you. Acknowledge that there isn't a magic bullet or just one way to manage others. Instead, be authentic and balance people and task concerns to quickly win the respect of others.

▲ Be humble. Admit when you don't know the answers – then go and find them. Similarly, know when to embrace failure and don't be afraid to pull the plug on a project if needed.

Inspiration

✦ Be a brilliant communicator – pure and simple. Excel at translating lofty strategy into meaningful activities. Help others to make sense of, and adapt to, their changing work environment. Know the right thing to say: read *Great Answers to Tough Questions at Work* by Michael Dodd.[200]

- Read up on Robert Rosenthal and Lenore Jacobson's 'Pygmalion effect'.[201] Consider the implications of these landmark experiments into the observer expectancy effect and how they could influence your own approach to motivating your team.

- Focus on each person's strengths and try to manage around any weaknesses. Help people to acknowledge their natural abilities and increase their flexibility by providing them with varied work experiences. Look up *Theory Z* by William Ouchi and find out how the adoption of non-specialised career paths can often build loyalty and greater longevity of employment.[202]

⚙️ Ideas for delivering results

Good management is the art of making problems so interesting and their solutions so constructive that everyone wants to get to work and deal with them.

Paul Hawken

Tools

- Build loyalty by appealing to universal drivers to keep your team motivated and engaged. Use the 5A's model. Agree their objectives. Allow them to perform their role. Appraise their performance. Assist them with support and development. Acknowledge their personal contribution.

- Know where you sit on the situational decision making continuum.[203] Do you prefer a greater degree of control over what happens, or are you more willing to release the reins to create more opportunities for delegated responsibility? Both styles have consequences.

■ If you work in, or are responsible for, a remote team or geographically disparate project group, why not introduce one of the many task management apps available to organise your projects and improve communication? Wunderlist, Basecamp and Huddle can all help people to work together and share information without a reliance on email.

Techniques

▲ Keep it simple. Making things complex for the sake of it disengages people and pushes them away. Follow the lead of Mary Barra, the CEO of General Motors, who replaced their prescriptive ten-page dress code in favour of two words which read 'dress appropriately'.

▲ Identify opportunities to instil a sense of energy, enthusiasm and excitement into your people. Most of the individuals you manage will have two things in common: a desire to come to work and feel they have done a good job, combined with a need to be recognised for doing so.

▲ Avoid complicated appraisal systems. Concentrate instead on how to engage each employee in a way that is meaningful to them. Great managers ask staff to track their own performance and record their successes and personal discoveries on a project-by-project basis.

▲ Foster collaboration while also encouraging personalisation. Provide each employee with the space and freedom to individualise their work area to build their morale and boost their connectivity with the work environment.

▲ Stop treating all members of the team the same. Contrary to popular thinking, treating the same isn't fair and it isn't particularly engaging. Instead, manage one person at a time. Develop them and their responsibilities based on their individual talents and abilities.

▲ Have more one-to-ones with all your team. Spend longer on every one-to-one and always try to avoid cancelling these meetings. Demonstrate to others that your time with them is your most valuable work activity. Involve people in the decisions which affect them.

14

- Watch out for the bystander effect when asking people to do something. Asking more than one person to complete a task will make it more likely that nobody will. Instead, select a single person to take on the responsibility.

- Don't habitualise your meetings. Communicate in abundance, but only pull people together for a purpose. When you do hold meetings, run them to the agreed timings, get the involvement of everyone present and rotate the facilitator's role.

- Help others to grow. Rethink traditional career paths. Identify opportunities to extend capability laterally by investigating alternative development methods, remembering to include your high commitment–high capability team members.

- Delegate to develop. Use delegation as one of your pivotal development tools. Pinpoint the task, identify the person, build milestones and agree support. Accept that when you do delegate, the other person may do it in a slightly different way to you. They may make mistakes and could (at first) take far more time to complete the task.

- Invite dissent. Create space for criticism and welcome alternative viewpoints. Run a short monthly forum for people to look at barriers to success and air any frustrations. Communicate that it is okay to challenge the status quo in a constructive way. Supplement your personal understanding based on the insights received from others.

- Get out of the way. Default to trust. Be accessible and visible, but don't micro-manage. Provide people with permission. It builds commitment and inspires better performance.

14

Inspiration

- Invest in a copy of *First, Break All the Rules* by Marcus Buckingham and Curt Coffman and discover why the ability to individualise may be the most valuable skill any manager can possess. According to extensive research by Gallup, this one elusive quality is shared by all successful managers, enabling them to effectively balance both people and task concerns in order to deliver exceptional results. Read the book to find out more.[204]

- Be a virgin. Follow the Branson lead and adopt a high support–high challenge model to stretch your people and encourage personal growth. Provide radically candid feedback and learn how to 'care personally and challenge directly'. Find out more by reading *Radical Candor* by Kim Scott.[205]

- Read *The Silent Language of Leaders* by Carol Kinsey Goman to identify the two sets of body language cues which people look for in great leaders.[206] One set projects warmth and supportiveness; the other signals power and status.

- Promote partnerships and collaborative enterprise. Reinforce the importance of cooperation by watching Yves Morieux's TED Talk 'Too Many Rules at Work Keep You from Getting Things Done'.[207]

- Be a giant. Recruit people who have the potential to be better than you. Have the confidence to be surrounded by exceptional people and elevate your status by managing effective teams. As David Ogilvy, founder of Ogilvy & Mather, famously once said, 'If each of us hires people who are smaller than we are, we shall become a company of dwarfs. But if each of us hires people who are bigger than we are, we shall become a company of giants.'[208]

Ideas for long-term gain

A leader is best when people barely know he exists. Not so good when people obey him and acclaim him. Worse when they despise him. But of a good leader, who talks little, when his work is done, his aim fulfilled, they will say, 'We did this ourselves'.

Lao-Tse

14

Tool

▪ Take a walk. Spend more time with the people who have direct responsibility for different work functions to your own. Do a Gemba.[209] Undertake a structured visit, walking the length of the process or the service. The Gemba encourages managers to ask a series of questions such as, 'What are you doing now?' and 'What challenges do you face?' The aim of these walks is to understand and improve the systems, work methods and experience of the people delivering the work.

Techniques

▲ Champion continuous improvement by celebrating creativity and innovation in the workplace. Reward inventiveness and new approaches. Be action centred in your approach and demonstrate an unyielding commitment to focusing on applied solutions.

▲ Acknowledge the notion that involved workers are the key. Apply a democratic leadership style with collective decision making to deliver improved performance.

▲ Accept that you will have to make unpopular decisions to move forward. Constructively address conflict in order to progress and build confidence in your ability to challenge upwards – questioning your own managers if required.

▲ Know your demographics. Recognise that Generation Z's will soon be the most represented group in the working population. Gen Z's want to learn for themselves, they are comfortable challenging established practices and they are likely to respond better to collaborative leadership styles.

▲ Remember to be vulnerable. Sometimes, all the effort we put into showing how strong we are actually diminishes our position. Being vulnerable can be a sign of strength, not a sign of weakness. Acknowledge your fallibility. Practise asking for help more often, without adding any conditions to your request. Try using 'Can you help me?' to build trust and respect.

14

▲ Be much less tolerant. Reflect on the statement that the culture of any organisation will always be shaped by the worst behaviour the leader is willing to tolerate.

Inspiration

✦ Redefine your role as a catalyst and coach to others and use every opportunity to extend the performance of those around you. Encourage others to favour ongoing feedback over process driven annual performance reviews. Search for 'Google, Project Oxygen' and then apply the eight traits of a stellar manager to your own role.

✦ Don't focus on what to do; instead concentrate on what to stop doing. Dip into *What Got You Here Won't Get You There* by Marshall Goldsmith and discover concrete tips on how to spot your weaker areas and then start fixing them.[210]

✦ Apply a little science. Find some unexpected ways to take control of your psychological machinery and sharpen your personal performance by following the advice in *The Leading Brain: Powerful Science-Based Strategies for Achieving Peak Performance* by Friederike Fabritius and Hans Hagemann.[211]

 # Related work skills

 14

Ability to Influence (1), Commitment to Change and Adaptation (3), Constructive Communication (4), Effective Planning and Organisation (7), Focus on Developing Others (9), Motivation to Succeed (12), Positive Decisions (15), Resilience and Emotional Control (17), Teamwork and Collaboration (20).

KEY 15

Positive Decisions

Positive Decisions

People who make positive decisions demonstrate a commitment to reach a resolution and initiate action. They are able to think on their feet and will evaluate evolving circumstances and make adjustments to ensure success. These individuals will consider a range of alternatives and then act with confidence to reach an informed conclusion. They excel at drawing on the opinions of others and will accommodate different views to assist with the decision making process. Generally, they will assess risk effectively by staying informed and are likely to have a capacity for overcoming any apparent barriers to success. They readily take ownership of issues and can make sound judgements in a timely fashion.

 ## Ideas for personal development

> *Choices are the hinges of destiny.*
>
> **Edwin Markham**

Tools

15

- Start with a simple decision making tool such as the Winston Churchill balance sheet method for more straightforward 'Should I?/Shouldn't I?' situations. On one half of a blank page write down all the reasons not to go ahead; on the other half write down all the reason to adopt the proposal. Review both sides.

- Plan for doomsday. Understand the risks associated with the decision you have made. Consider the absolute worst-case scenario, then plan ways to mitigate against this situation. Practise applying Balaam's strategy to create more informed decisions. Look at all the alternatives through a more negative lens. Criticise each item in turn by considering all the obstacles to implementation. Review each barrier in turn and try to overcome them. Finally, select your preferred solution.

▦ Think of a specific decision you need to make. Draw a large six-pointed star. Write the title of the issue you are faced with in the centre of the star. At each of the six points write one of the following: who, what, when, where, how and why, and then answer each in turn to help shape your decision making process.

Techniques

▲ Flex your decision making muscle. Strengthen it by making more of them. Studies show that you are more likely to make things happen by accepting uncertainty and avoiding the temptation to over-plan or dwell on technicalities.[212] Own all of your decisions. If you genuinely believe something is the right thing to do, then fully commit to your choice and take the lead by owning the consequences if things don't go to plan.

▲ Ask an expert. Every decision you are thinking about will more than likely have been made by someone else at some point. Seek them out and learn from their experience.

▲ Resist making any direct association between the decisions you make and the results you obtain, as there are usually lots of variables involved. It's often hard for us to accept that a positive outcome may simply be the product of a random effect. Evidence suggests that the results we achieve will always be influenced by many more factors than just our initial decision to proceed.[213]

▲ Avoid decision making fatigue. Consider the relationship between your personal energy levels and the quality of the decisions you are making. Studies of parole board court rulings reveal that the judge's level of fatigue at the time any ruling was made played a significant role on the final verdict. Generally speaking, the longer the day went on, the more the chances of a favourable ruling dropped.[214]

Inspiration

+ Recognise that while wisdom comes from taking many perspectives, you cannot make a decision and move forwards unless you can differentiate between options. Google 'Buridan's ass' or investigate Robert Kane's analysis in *A Contemporary Introduction to Free Will* to find out about the significance of this statement.[215]

+ Get angry. Quality decisions often use three different processes – analysing, imagining and valuing. Watch the classic decision making film *12 Angry Men* (1957) and identify where each of these processes influenced what happened at the trial.

+ Find out what is important – and stick with it. Read *Essentialism* by Greg McKeown and learn ways to be more selective to enable you to focus on the vital few decisions which actually need to be made.[216] Apply proven methods to simplify all your tasks and discover new techniques to keep your energies concentrated on where they will have the greatest impact.

⚙ Ideas for delivering results

> *If you're offered a seat on a rocket ship, don't ask what seat.*
>
> **Sheryl Sandberg**

15

Tools

▦ To encourage a participative approach to decision making, why not try Kurt Lewin's force field analysis in your next team meeting. Ask your peers to identify all of the driving forces and all of the restraining forces before assigning a weighting to each item. For any change to take place, the driving forces must be strengthened or the restraining forces weakened.

- Learn from a fighter pilot and discover how to make better decisions under pressure. Investigate and apply John Boyd's OODA loop model to help you to organise your thought process, adapt to changing circumstances and improve the quality of your decision making.[217] The more rapidly you can move through the Observe, Orient, Decide, Act cycle (and then repeat this four-step loop), the more effective your final decision is likely to become.

- For the rationally minded, try using a USER-bility calculation to help you decide between a range of similar options. Simply rate each item from 1 to 3 (low to high) for each of the following categories: Use of your talents, Scale of impact, Ease of implementation and Relevance to existing goals. Then multiply the results of all four variables to reveal a value figure for each of your options.

Techniques

- If you are pragmatic by nature and are more focused on delivering outcomes, be conscious that you may be inclined to adopt the first workable solution – which may not always be the most effective one. Try not to just fix the broken bits and work around the issue. Test it, trial it, pilot it and try it out in a safe environment. Secure feedback, revise it and test it again.

- Distance yourself from your dilemma. Remind yourself about the importance of being rational. It sounds too flimsy to work, but taking time out to stop and deliberately acknowledge to yourself the need to be more dispassionate has been found to improve the quality of the final decision made. Additionally, imagining yourself as a third party onlooker who is making the same decision will often improve the quality of the decision.[218]

- Become a master of TPN. For each sub-task, identify as early as possible whether the required actions are Totally, Partially or Not at all within your control. Focus on what you can influence and where you can bridge solutions. Gain support for all the rest.

- Beware of vivid, emphatic and personalised requests. It is easy to be swayed by emotive appeals.

▲ Try to avoid voting on important issues where possible. Deciding by majority rule can be expedient, but it doesn't build commitment to the decision by those people outvoted by others; instead, it creates groups of winners and losers.

▲ Consult with your polar opposite. Ask the advice of a colleague who normally has a totally different take on things to yourself. Differences between people can create traction for more informed decisions.

▲ Always question your evidence base. Use statistics with caution. Correlation doesn't equal causation.[219] Consider the sample sizes and reference groups used to support any claims.

▲ Build commitment to important decisions by involving others in a process of decision making through facilitated consensus. Embrace the voice of the 'lone wolf'. Groupthink suffocates innovation, so welcome diverse ideas and viewpoints.

▲ Improve your decision making by recognising your default preferences. Do you tend to favour decisions which will impact on the here and now, or do you usually look to play the long game? According to the theory of processing fluency, decisions which are easier for us to process are far more likely to be approved. They are easier to follow and this fluency of mental processing makes us feel good.[220]

▲ Explore the principles of parallel thinking and discover ways to consider important decisions from a variety of perspectives.[221] Minimise the risk of adversarial approaches and encourage the adoption of more inventive solutions.

▲ Acknowledge the advantages of sometimes making no decision at all, rather than reinventing the wheel for its own sake. Postpone some things until later to focus on what is important now. Adopt a 'not now, but later' approach for certain tasks.

▲ Conduct 'what if?' scenarios. Try out risk specific simulations to improve both operational and strategic decision making.

▲ Get onto cloud nine and evaluate the significance. If you are struggling to decide whether something is really pressing or not, ask yourself if this issue will still matter in nine minutes, nine hours, nine days, nine weeks or even nine months? If it will truly matter for all of these, then pay attention to it. If not, consider focusing on things that will bring greater value and get on with something else. Always commit resources which are proportionate to the overall impact of the decision.

Inspiration

+ Commit to buying better books. Get hold of a copy of *Decisive: How to Make Better Decisions* by Chip and Dan Heath and discover ways to find robust solutions by avoiding any reliance on instinctive reactions and faulty thinking.[222]

+ Remember all decisions are not born equal. Don't sweat the small stuff. Become effective at making speedier decisions about everyday choices which have little long-term effect on you or others. Automate or habitualise trivial and unimportant decisions to increase your mental capacity to process more information by filtering out the unimportant stuff. Apple co-founder Steve Jobs wore virtually identical versions of the same clothing and footwear every day for more than a decade to minimise the number of decisions he had to make in unimportant areas. Barack Obama only wore two suit colours to free up his own mental space.[223]

+ Find out what great decision makers do differently and how to avoid the three most common decision making traps by watching Benedikt Ahlfeld's TEDx Talk 'The Power of Decision-Making'.[224]

+ Postpone tough decisions until after lunch. According to a study from Columbia Business School, you should try to leave any difficult choices you have to make until after you've eaten. Replenishing your energy and feeling more refreshed will make you better prepared to tackle complex decisions. Discover more temporal tips to optimise your daily routines by reading *When: The Scientific Secrets of Perfect Timing* by Daniel Pink.[225]

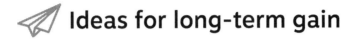

Ideas for long-term gain

> *… you can't make decisions based on fear and the possibility of what might happen.*
>
> **Michelle Obama**

Tools

▪ Complete the SHL CEB Fastrack test and receive reliable and valid feedback on your decision making abilities. Fastrack is a robust psychometric test which assesses your potential to acquire and process information. It has been demonstrated to be beneficial to anyone interested in extending their decision making performance.

▪ Tap into the wisdom of a group of experts, but prevent them from influencing each other by practising a simplified version of the Delphi method, which is useful for larger, more complex issues where time is not a critical factor.[226]

Techniques

▲ Decentralise the decision making process. Invariably, the people closest to the problem will be best placed to solve it. Provide them with greater knowledge of all the issues and then empower them with the responsibility for developing the solutions.

▲ Keep testing the waters. Check the temperature – regularly. Assess the wider organisational climate by using short, frequent and informal mini-surveys to evaluate engagement levels and provide indications as to how your decisions may be received. Fear-based cultures can drive short-term instrumental decision making, while risk averse environments are likely to resist radical change.

▲ Become an accountant. Evaluate viability. Use a four-quadrant cost–value matrix to compare the financial impact of different proposals. This is particularly useful when looking to identify the feasibility of new ventures and customer driven innovations.

▲ Balance the rational with the intuitive. Know when to use logic and when to rely on your instincts by differentiating between puzzles and mysteries. Numerous studies confirm that puzzles tend to have clear answers and require more rational processes to solve them. Mysteries are more complex and benefit from less logical approaches such as intuition.[227]

▲ For larger decisions, establish a timetable for carrying out the decision making process. Create three to six milestones and map these against the timeline. Examples could include: 'Analyse situation by …', 'Clarify goals by …', 'Identify alternatives by …' and 'Decide between options by …' Share your timetable with everyone who has the potential to be impacted by the decision.

Inspiration

✦ Splash out on an updated edition of *Predictably Irrational* by Dan Ariely and see how easy it is to have our rational thinking processes manipulated (and what to do about it).[228]

✦ Search out philosopher Ruth Chang's TED Talk 'How to Make Hard Choices'.[229] In just fourteen minutes you will understand her practical framework for how to make some of the hardest decisions that we all face in life.

✦ Don't worry about making the wrong decision. Face up to the possibility of failure and embrace your mistakes. Read *Black Box Thinking: Marginal Gains and the Secrets of High Performance* by Matthew Syed and learn how to how to jump in, commit to your decision and move forward.[230]

Related work skills

Commercial Thinking (2), Creativity and Innovation (5), Direction and Purpose (6), Effective Planning and Organisation (7), Intuitive Thought (11), People Management and Leadership Potential (14), Resilience and Emotional Control (17), Use of Information and Data (21).

Professional Ethics and Social Responsibility

Professional Ethics and Social Responsibility

People who are ethically and socially responsible will aim for a consistency between their expressed principles and their personal approach. They are likely to demonstrate respect and positive regard for the values of others and will aim to promote a positive, tolerant and welcoming atmosphere. Typically, they embrace employee welfare concerns and will promote an ethos of service and contribution at work. Highly trusted as individuals, they have strong professional integrity and will strive to build diverse teams. They hold themselves and others accountable for their actions. Inclusive by approach, they tell the truth and are honest in their dealings. By considering the wider social and moral implications of their actions, they are able to forge constructive networks within the local community.

 ## Ideas for personal development

Differences challenge assumptions.

Anne Wilson Schaef

Tool

16

- Benchmark your own ethical approach, and those of your peers, using Rizzardi's summary of professional ethics which states: 'the core essence of professionalism can be expressed as follows: character, competence, commitment, and courtesy.'[231]

Techniques

▲ Form your own personal code. Define your values. Acknowledge what is important to you and what you represent. Aim for a consistency between your expressed principles and your personal approach. Compare your values to those of the organisation.

▲ Where possible, separate yourself from the opinion of others. It is liberating to discover you are not always in control of your own reputation. All you can control is yourself and how you act on a day-to-day basis. Recognise that you are responsible for treating others fairly, honestly and with respect for their dignity.

▲ Track down a copy of the professional standards document for your position or industry. Most occupations and sectors adhere to a clearly defined set of professional standards. What are yours?

▲ Watch your step. Be mindful of the immediate office environment – not just in terms of potential trips and slips hazards, but also making sure it is clean, comfortable, well-lit and welcoming to others.

▲ Show your support for worthwhile causes and, where possible, contribute to fundraising activities. Start simple – run a charity event or fundraising challenge. Get in touch with a local voluntary organisation. Find an area which interests you and offer your support or services, even on a trial basis.

▲ Join your local health and welfare workgroup (or health and safety committee) and add value by representing the everyday concerns of your peers.

▲ Develop a reputation as someone who acknowledges the variety of differing interests and agendas across the organisation and is also capable of reconciling accepted office politics through a desire to 'do the right thing'.

16

Inspiration

✛ Ethics are usually more powerful than rules. There is an old Zen saying which states that whatever you are for strengthens you, and whatever you are against weakens you. Stop to consider what it is you stand for.

✛ Give a little. Find out about the new currency of success in *Give and Take* by Adam Grant.[232] Discover how being an 'otherish-giver' could provide you with a new perspective on personal success.

⚙ Ideas for delivering results

Your reputation and integrity are everything. Follow through on what you say you're going to do. Your credibility can only be built over time and it is built from the history of your words and actions.

Maria Razumich-Zec

Tools

▪ Confront your personal bias. We all tend to believe that we have fewer biases than the average person. Research demonstrates that the more objective people think they are, the more likely they are to unknowingly discriminate, because they don't realise how vulnerable they are to bias.[233] Search online for the Implicit Association Test to discover your own hidden attitudes, beliefs and unconscious biases.

▪ Recognise and account for cultural diversity across your organisation. Two methods to explore existing organisational culture include the Graves Model (or Spiral Dynamics)[234] and the Organizational Culture Inventory (OCI) from Human Synergistics International.

Techniques

▲ Operate with transparency. Be respectful of confidentiality when dealing with others on an interpersonal level, both in terms of personal disclosures and access to any restricted or sensitive information.

▲ Protect your integrity. Be impeccable with your word. Keep commitments, fulfil your promises and express your thoughts and feelings clearly, saying no when you need to. Always be accountable. Stand tall and be counted for the actions you have undertaken and their consequences – good and bad.

▲ Choose to associate with colleagues who have outstanding personal integrity. Their personal definitions of what is right and wrong may sometimes differ from your own, but the way they remain true to their ideals may create a lasting bond.

▲ Decide on how you want to contribute on a personal level. It could be by operating in a more sustainable way, leaving the car at home, treating others well, supporting environmentally friendly products or giving to worthwhile causes. Furthermore, research has found that being more generous can make you a happier person.[235]

▲ Be an ambassador for a spirit of service and contribution. Demonstrate your approach by being supportive and loyal to others who can offer you no immediate gain. Share your admiration for colleagues who consider wider social and moral implications.

▲ Get more informed. Follow the latest developments in all matters relating to fairness, access, equality and social inclusion. Talk to HR and see if they run a working group which you could join. Access a specialist speaker on ethical practices for your team through the Institute of Business Ethics.

▲ Focusing solely on difference in the workplace may increase rather than decrease feelings of social exclusion for some less represented groups. Research from Yale suggests that concentrating mainly on variance may inadvertently emphasise an individual's distinctness.[236] Focus instead on

16

driving inclusivity by encouraging both a sense of belonging and a feeling of uniqueness by helping all your people to feel connected to their colleagues and also recognised for their distinct qualities.

- Develop a well-considered code of ethics. Make it sector specific and avoid vague statements such as 'Be professional'. Include the detail, but don't make it too long.

- Reinforce your ethical stance and any behavioural expectations at all stages of the employee lifecycle. Include a short section on your organisational values during inductions and have conversations about behavioural elements during performance management discussions.

- Become a deontologist. According to deontology, decisions are morally sound if they are based on adherence to an accepted and overriding moral principle which was developed through informed reasoning.

- Get everyone involved in a professional ethics workshop, providing a range of ethical cases and situations for people to explore and comment on. This is particularly useful when combined with an exploration of evolving organisational values.

- Strike the pose. Propose an ethical conundrum for colleagues to comment on at your next team meeting, add the dilemma to a blog and encourage people to talk more openly about more ethical issues as part of their everyday conversations.

Inspiration

- Make it matter. Bury yourself in a copy of *The Power of Meaning: The True Route to Happiness* by Emily Esfahani Smith and find out why we often lose meaning in our lives and what we can do about it – both in the workplace and in the wider community.[237]

- If any of your colleagues think they are too small to make a difference, remind them of the founder of the Body Shop, the late Anita Roddick, who once said, 'If you think you're too small to have an impact, try going to bed with a mosquito in the room.'

- Read more books which reveal the social realities of the wider developing world. Try *I Am Malala* by Malala Yousafzai[238] or *Sold* by Patricia McCormick.[239] Immediately challenge any examples of oppressive and discriminatory practices in your workplace.

- Search for accessibilitypartners.com and investigate their aim to make information technology more accessible to people with disabilities. Next, discuss with colleagues how a more proactive approach could be applied in your workplace.

- Consider whether or not ethical practice is simply monkey business. Watch Frans de Waal's 'Moral Behaviour in Animals' TEDx Talk and see just how many of our responses to fairness, reciprocity and empathy are, in fact, shared with other mammals.[240]

- Watch the 'Ethics for People on the Move' TEDx Talk by Catharyn Baird and learn how to ask the right questions to build stronger communities.[241]

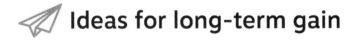 # Ideas for long-term gain

Shelving hard decisions is the least ethical course.

Adrian Cadbury

Tool

- Visit a micro-lending portal such as kiva.org and discover how easy it is to make a socially responsible loan of a few pounds which could help to launch an otherwise socially excluded business in another part of the world.

16

Techniques

▲ Where possible, encourage transparency of pay across your entire organisation. Evidence suggests that freely sharing salary information makes for a more productive and engaging workplace, plus it is easier to avoid gender-based pay differentials and other forms of discrimination. Research author David Burkus for more details.

▲ Decide on how you want to contribute on an organisational level. Consumers are more likely to buy from a company which supports and engages in activities to improve society.[242] Support doesn't need to be financial in nature; it could be providing assistance through technical knowledge to a local charity – allowing them to use your resources during quieter times. Give back to the wider community.

▲ Forget about donations. The most effective social responsibility programmes encourage a two-way relationship between organisations and the community they are involved with, to enable them to grow and develop together. Take a positive stance towards positively affecting the people and environments outside of your immediate organisation. Champion the development of an organisational policy towards corporate social responsibility.

▲ Recognise the advantages that neurodiverse people can bring to your workplace. Actively embrace neurological differences such as dyspraxia, dyslexia, attention deficit hyperactivity disorder and Tourette's, in the same way as any other human variation. A recent Harvard study concluded that neurodiversity in the workplace can provide a competitive edge for companies.[243]

▲ Join a network group like Business in the Community to share best practice and innovative approaches towards building a fairer society and a sustainable future.

▲ Create a short set of ethical guidelines for all your suppliers. Look at their credentials and encourage everyone who trades with you to, for example, cut down on any unnecessary packaging. Document ways to collectively pursue your common values.

16

Inspiration

+ Learn to lead with good character in any situation. Get hold of a copy of *Good People* by Anthony Tjan and discover practical ways to develop a values-based culture which will translate into long-term success.[244]

+ Encourage senior managers to recognise that social responsibility initiatives can often reduce costs by focusing on ecological concerns, recycling and reducing your carbon footprint. Investment in community-based activities can also provide excellent marketing and public relations (PR) opportunities to help build your reputation as an employer of choice. Search the web to find out how Yvon Chouinard transformed Patagonia's fortunes by focusing on environmental conservation.

+ Be good to yourself and others by taking a leaf out of Sweden's book. Read up on *lagom* and apply some of the principles for a happier, more egalitarian and community-based approach to the world around you.

 Related work skills

Commercial Thinking (2), Direction and Purpose (6), Enthusiasm for Customer Service (8), Focus on Developing Others (9), Specialist Knowledge and Ability (19).

16

Resilience and Emotional Control

Resilience and Emotional Control

People who demonstrate resilience and emotional control express a firmness of purpose and can work with commitment and enthusiasm to achieve important goals. They are inclined to believe in their own capabilities. These flexible individuals are able to handle big workloads, competing demands, interruptions and distractions with poise and ease. They can think clearly under pressure and have the capacity to remain calm and composed. Mentally robust, they tend to view most obstacles as challenges to be met and are not demotivated by setbacks or changing circumstances. They know when to seek the support of others to help overcome adverse situations. Capable of managing their own emotions and impulses, they are likely to regard any personal criticism as an opportunity to learn and improve.

 ## Ideas for personal development

> *Be curious. And however difficult life may seem, there is always something you can do, and succeed at. It matters that you don't just give up.*
>
> **Stephen Hawking**

Tool

17

■ Acknowledge all of your signature strengths. Too often we are encouraged to focus on our limitations and so may forget to acknowledge everything at which we excel. Try out the free Character Strengths survey at viacharacter.org. To understand your personal strengths and preferences and how best to apply them, investigate Gretchen Rubin's Four Tendencies framework and take her tendencies quiz at gretchenrubin.com.[245]

Techniques

▲ Pump up your personal positivity. Resilient people are far more likely to identify little pockets of silver linings even in the worst of circumstances. Being more optimistic is not only closely linked to higher levels of personal resilience, but it is also a mental state which can be learned and mastered – regardless of your genetic make-up.[246] Watch Tali Sharot's TED Talk 'The Optimism Bias' to discover the benefits of training your brain to zoom in on positive events.[247]

▲ Get enough sleep and plenty of exercise to ensure you are able to cope effectively with all the challenges in your life. Mental breaks and deliberate calm can keep stress chemicals at bay, reducing the potential for feeling overwhelmed.

▲ Reward small wins. Resilient people have self-belief, they work hard, persevere and take pleasure in small wins which bring personal satisfaction.

▲ Be more grey. Avoid black-and-white thinking and apply a more graduated approach. Avoiding all-or-nothing thinking supports the exploration of creative options.

▲ Avoid the drama. Office gossip fires up your emotional centre and can knock you off balance. Be empathetic and compassionate, but don't worry about what others think of you or defer to peer pressure against your better judgement.

▲ Learn to trust. Being sceptical about other people's intentions may limit your ability to draw on social support when you need it. Defer dialogue – hold back from expressing your views and opinions until you have heard everyone else and you fully understand the situation. Remain open, rather than react from a position of opinion and judgement.

Inspiration

+ Hunt for a copy of *The Impossible Just Takes a Little Longer* by Art Berg – essential reading for anyone interested in how to overcome adversity.[248] If you are short of time, search for the poem 'Don't Quit' by John Greenleaf Whittier.

+ Face life's problems head-on. In his book *The Obstacle is the Way*, Ryan Holiday provides techniques to turn adversity into advantage, suggesting that overcoming challenges is one of the most effective ways to grow.[249]

+ Learn to juggle – literally. Activities which require focus and practice strengthen the frontal lobe and support higher level thinking.[250] Alternatively, get a hobby which will enable you to recharge your batteries. Warren Buffet loves playing the ukulele. Bill Gates plays lots of bridge. Try to schedule purposeful downtime into each day.

⚙ Ideas for delivering results

The best survivors spend almost no time, especially in emergencies, getting upset about what has been lost, or feeling distressed about things going badly. … For this reason they don't usually take themselves too seriously and are therefore hard to threaten.

Al Siebert

Tools

▪ Lighten up. When you do feel under pressure, find a moment to visit Spotify and listen to 'Weightless' by Marconi Union. This music has been specially designed with sound therapists to promote a feeling of relaxation, and evidence suggests it may significantly reduce both anxiety levels and blood pressure.[251]

17

Search for meaning. Develop a 'personal why' statement. Having your own compass will provide a clear sense of purpose and will help you to view any setbacks from a broader perspective.

Techniques

Define your goals, make sure they match your personal values and then pursue them relentlessly. Resilient people view stretching goals as a challenge, not an obstacle. Identify compelling reasons to get involved and be proactive.

Study at the school of stoicism. Try not to dwell on events and situations which are outside your control. Identify the things you can influence and invest your time and energy here. Fail fast and move on quickly. Learn from the event and let go. Adapt quickly to new developments by being curious and asking lots of questions.

Mange any stress using distraction and resolution methods. Distraction includes exercise, breathing techniques, walking and extracting yourself from the situation. Resolution is focused on solving the problem.

Take a cold bath. If you can't remove the stressors, build up your ability to deal with them. Studies reveal that taking a cold bath in the morning (or cold water swimming) increases mental toughness and your ability to face stressful situations.[252]

Exercise self-control. Look up Walter Mischel's iconic 'marshmallow test' and discover the relationship between deferred gratification and success in everyday life.[253] Personal willpower is in limited supply. There is a greater chance of giving in to instant gratification and impulsive behaviour when you are mentally exhausted.

Helping others is recognised as a powerful way of enhancing mental toughness. Multiple acts of kindness have been found to have a cumulative positive effect on our mental toughness.[254] Extend your personal resilience by bolstering the confidence levels of colleagues who are less resilient than you.

- Connect with others across your organisation. Research reveals that strong social connections bolster resilience, increase well-being and make you feel more productive.[255] Begin noticing who you spend time with on a daily basis. If you are connecting with people who are optimistic and more satisfied with life, you will start to be affected by their positive outlook.[256]

- Practise seeing things from another person's point of view. When we empathise with others, we feel less isolated, less entrenched in our own problems and are able to recover more quickly.

Inspiration

- Become an osteologist. According to All Blacks coach Gilbert Enoka, 'you need only three bones to be successful: a wish bone, a back bone, and a funny bone'. The wishbone emphasises the importance of having a goal. The back bone means having the courage to see things through. The funny bone reminds us of the importance of not taking ourselves too seriously.

- Be more courageous, more vulnerable, more connected and more resilient. Identify practical ways to show up, speak up, act and fail more often by reading *Daring Greatly* by Brene Brown.[257]

- Embrace your stress. Hear how the latest research on the biology of courage is suggesting that stress may only be bad for you if you believe it to be the case. Watch Kelly McGonigal's compelling TED Talk on 'How to Make Stress Your Friend'.[258]

- Mind yourself. Read *Mindfulness: A Practical Guide to Finding Peace in a Frantic World* by Mark Williams and Danny Penman.[259] Apply their down-to-earth methods to reduce personal anxiety and stress and build a happier, more confident approach to your working life.

- Identify a personal resilience role model. Select someone who oozes bouncebackability. Monitor their reactions in social situations and try to mirror their approach. Next, read *Grit* by Angela Duckworth and discover the significance of the combined power of passion and perseverance, plus an effective way to focus your energy on your five highest priority goals.[260]

17

- Download a podcast by Srikumar Rao on how to be more resilient at work – he offers heaps of practical ideas for entrepreneurs and employees.

- Resist perfectionism. It may be a form of procrastination and prevent you from moving forward with things. Eighty per cent is good enough in most cases. Avoid the roadblocks by reading *The War of Art* by Steve Pressfield.[261]

- Watch Isaac Lidsky's TED Talk 'What Reality Are You Creating for Yourself?' and discover some great ideas on how to let go of excuses, assumptions and fears.[262]

- Endure more. Get more out of yourself and others by reading Alex Hutchinson's scientific dive into the limits of human performance. Grab a copy of *Endure* and discover precisely what it is that successful athletes do to keep pushing forwards against a mounting desire to stop.[263]

- Train your chimp to manage your emotions. Understand your mind and where many of your impulsive responses come from. Read *The Chimp Paradox* by Steve Peters and apply proven scientific principles to gain greater control of your thinking and make better decisions on a daily basis.[264]

Ideas for long-term gain

> *… a certain amount of opposition is a great help to a man. Kites rise against, and not with, the wind.*
>
> **John Neal**

17

Tools

- Complete a MTQ48 mental toughness inventory and review your results for levels of challenge, control, commitment and confidence.[265]

- Investigate the Stockdale paradox and then apply this principle to your most challenging work issue.[266]

Techniques

- Improve your decision making. Resilience requires you to make more decisions rather than avoid them. This means you should trust your judgement – but don't be averse to changing your mind.

- Exercise impulse control – practise techniques to resist or delay an impulse, drive or temptation to act.

- Make things tougher for yourself. Baseball players practise swinging with a weighted bat so that batting feels easier during real games.[267] In the same way, you can increase your personal stamina by stretching yourself more. Try deliberately increasing one of your personal targets on a specific day each week and monitor the results.

- Make more promises – and keep them. Hardy people have greater capacity, make more realistic plans and take steps to carry them out.

Inspiration

- Watch the inspirational TEDx Talk by Sam Berns entitled 'My Philosophy for a Happy Life'.[268]

- Introduce an idea generation exercise at your next team meeting based on a famous quote by performance psychologist Jim Loehr. Ask people for three suggestions on how best to 'consistently perform towards the upper range of [their] talent and skill regardless of competitive circumstances'.[269] Take note of their responses and act on them.

17

- Develop your emotional literacy. Practise reducing any unwanted emotional arousal by consciously recognising your own emotional states. Discover reliable ways to do this using David Rock's book *Your Brain at Work*: 'To reduce arousal, you need to use just a few words to describe an emotion, and ideally use symbolic language, which means using indirect metaphors, metrics, and simplifications of your experience'.[270]

- Practise 'prospective hindsight' by using the pre-mortem technique to look ahead and anticipate any potential future issues. Find out more by watching Daniel Levitin's TED Talk 'How to Stay Calm When You Know You'll Be Stressed'.[271]

 ## Related work skills

Commitment to Change and Adaptation (3), Enthusiasm for Customer Service (8), Interpersonal Awareness and Diplomacy (10), Intuitive Thought (11), Ownership of Self-Development (13), People Management and Leadership Potential (14), Positive Decisions (15).

Results through Action

Results through Action

People who focus on the delivery of results through action make things happen. They invest in the accomplishment of recognised outcomes and take the initiative to generate worthwhile activity. Typically, they demonstrate a positive personal mindset and will create intentions for themselves which are realistic, challenging and action centred. They set stretching targets and work relentlessly to achieve them, pushing themselves and others to reach agreed milestones. These individuals concentrate their efforts on the identification of workable solutions and will overcome any setbacks to move forwards. They are likely to be energetic and persistent and will go the extra mile to complete tasks on time and in full. By striving to deliver performance excellence, they are able to identify what is and what is not relevant to the realisation of results. They have a capacity for the achievement of superior standards by balancing both productivity and quality requirements.

Ideas for personal development

> *The way to get started is to quit talking and begin doing.*
>
> **Walt Disney**

Tools

- Apply the action formula $O = E \times R$ to all your endeavours, where Outcomes are dictated by Events multiplied by your Response to them. Recognise the impact your thought processes and beliefs have on the results you achieve. You are in charge.

18

■ Work, eat, sleep, repeat. Establish effective routines for yourself to make it easier to achieve your goals. Track how well you are doing using a free habit building and productivity app such as HabitBull. Confirm the habits you would like to introduce and then receive handy reminders to ensure you stick to your goals. Other options include HabitHub, Loop and Habitica.

Techniques

▲ Before you can deliver any results, clarify what it is that needs delivering. Ask: where are we now? What does here look like? How did we get here? What is wrong with where we are? What prevents us from getting to where we want to be? What is the real problem? Ask for specifics and get a clear image of what the end result is expected to look like.

▲ Throw some more light on the situation. Simply working closer to natural light sources has been proven to improve your sense of well-being and, in turn, increases productivity levels.[272]

▲ Get uncomfortable. Make a deliberate effort to step out of your comfort zone at least once a day. However small, take action and try new things, new foods, new music and new work processes. Create a mindset where you are more comfortable with stepping into the unknown.

▲ Get supplemental. Ditch the cup of coffee and look into yerba mate, a natural plant used to help people stay alert. Made from South American rainforest holly trees, the calorie-free beverage can increase concentration and energy levels and is also packed with vitamins E, A and C.

▲ Be a completionist. Unfinished items on your to-do list may result in increased stress because of the Zeigarnik effect, which states that any unaddressed tasks will play on your mind until they are completed.[273] Investigate using a visible wall calendar to spread out activities over a longer time period.

18

Inspiration

+ Take action and make progress. Learn how to apply a proven system to achieve all your goals and reach your full potential by reading Michael Hyatt's *Your Best Year Ever*.[274] It is packed with real-life stories of ordinary people who have achieved extraordinary results.

+ Beat procrastination by changing your work environment, removing distractions and spending time with people who are industrious and purposeful. Overcome any barriers to success by watching Tim Urban's TED Talk 'Inside the Mind of a Master Procrastinator'.[275]

+ Overcome any complacency in the team by demonstrating a positive mental mindset and encourage others to do the same. Opportunity doesn't always knock. As the old adage goes, 'Opportunity is missed by most people because it is dressed in overalls and looks like work.'

⚙️ Ideas for delivering results

> *... it is in this whole process of meeting and solving problems that life has its meaning. Problems are the cutting edge that distinguishes between success and failure. ... Problems call forth our courage and our wisdom; indeed, they create our courage and our wisdom.*
>
> **Scott Peck**

Tools

▪ Research 'well-formed outcomes' and use this tool to develop your goals and those of your team.

18

From tiny acorns great oaks grow. Use ACORN to drive results. Firstly, Act as if you have already achieved the outcome – fully commit to believing it is possible. Next, Check – ensure you are on the right track by building in evaluation. Thirdly, Ownership – this must be 100 per cent. Fourthly, Resources – both now and what you can secure later. Finally, do it Now – set sail and stick with it.

Techniques

▲ Eat three frogs. Start your work by focusing on the three things which require a higher level of concentration or three things you don't want to do. Make a habit of eating three of these 'frogs' each and every morning to help overcome procrastination and preserve your mental energy.

▲ Recognise that motivation sometimes *follows* action. Motivation and drive can increase as you progress and gain feedback on your incremental movement. Contrary to popular wisdom, these may not always need to be present at the start of a project.

▲ Always be committed to the achievement of higher standards. Be dedicated to the delivery of operational excellence by subtly communicating a message that you are often pleased but rarely satisfied. Use solution orientated language: how did you know that? What happened next? What difference did this make?

▲ Work in short bursts. Apply the Pomodoro Technique to break up your work and keep your mind active – twenty-five minutes of uninterrupted work on a single task followed by a break of five minutes. Read Francesco Cirillo's book to discover the best ways to use this technique and transform how you work.[276]

▲ Investigate and apply different appropriate problem solving techniques to overcome any obstacles to success. Seek ever more effective ways to achieve your results. Introduce a plan–do–study–act model to reinforce a philosophy of continuous improvement.

18

- Multitasking as an effective work practice is a myth.[277] Where possible, abandon it. Winston Churchill is reported to have said, 'You will never reach your destination if you stop and throw stones at every dog that barks.' Be fully present and committed to a single task. The one possible exception to this is listening to podcasts and audiobooks while you are focused on a routine task such as exercising in the gym.

- Don't fixate too much on your expected outcomes. Focus on the next achievable milestone. No one ever runs towards a bus setting off half a mile away, but a bus pulling away thirty yards ahead is well worth chasing.

- Distinguish between problems and concerns. If a car breaks down because it has run out of fuel, this isn't a problem. It is a concern because you know how to resolve the situation. Problems are defined as such because we don't know what to do about them. Embrace problems.

- Add a little zest! Follow the example of a large Japanese firm which reduced the error rate of its keypad operators by almost 50 per cent by exposing them to the scent of lemons in the office.[278] Workplaces that are filled with indoor plants have also been found to boost attention and improve mood.[279] Painting your work environment in calming colours such as green and blue is also believed to improve efficiency and focus.

- Try to avoid analysis paralysis by shortening the thinking time. Consider the maxim, 'One ounce of action is worth a ton of theory.' Recognise that not knowing what to do is often worse than the work itself. Create a 'coming up next' list at the end of the day so you can hit the ground running every morning. Don't wait for the conditions to be ideal. Start just before you feel completely ready.

- Tamper with the thermostat. Researchers from Helsinki University of Technology discovered that human performance increases with temperatures between 69.8 and 71.6° Fahrenheit.[280] Chilly workers make more errors.

18

Inspiration

+ In some situations, talking about your ambitions to others could actually decrease your chances of achieving them. Watch the Derek Sivers TED Talk 'Keep Your Goals to Yourself' to find out more about this phenomenon.[281]

+ Search online for Vik Nithy for some great tips on how to overcome roadblocks when working on any new project.

+ Practise the power of one. Apply focus, block your time, eliminate distractions and stay on track.[282] Visit iTunes and download any of the free audio podcasts on 'The One Thing' by Geoff Woods, then read *Deep Work* by Cal Newport to uncover a range of simple rules to help you reclaim your powers of concentration, immerse yourself in any task and remain focused in an increasingly distracted world.[283]

+ Stand next to the brightest person in the room. Steve Jobs aligned himself to Steve Wozniak, Harold Ramis to Bill Murray and Bob Dylan was inspired by Woody Guthrie.

+ Be imperfect. Perfectionism is unrealistic in most work situations and may unknowingly be linked to delaying the achievement of outcomes. According to Henri-Frederic Amie, 'The man who insists upon seeing with perfect clearness before he decides, never decides.'

+ Watch Jason Fried's TED Talk 'Why Work Doesn't Happen at Work' and consider the environmental impact of where you work on the results you achieve.[284]

+ Question convention. Culturally, the UK tends to be more cautious in its decision making processes. It favours a Ready–Aim–Fire (RAF) model which is trusted yet risk averse. There are other Western cultures which advocate a Ready–Fire–Aim (RFA) approach. This second model is not about being reckless, but rather about undertaking planning and then going for it. If the target is missed first time, it doesn't matter because feedback is built in to the process, so the aim is simply adjusted and then another attempt made. Jim Collins and Morten Hansen advocate rapid prototyping with the advice 'fire bullets, then cannonballs' in their book *Great by Choice*.[285]

18

Ideas for long-term gain

Tool

- Appreciate more. Focus on the positive aspects of what is working well on your projects and key tasks by applying an Appreciative Inquiry (AI) framework to involve others, extend momentum and encourage more of the same.[286]

Techniques

- Resist any attempts to introduce payments by results schemes or similar incentives, and instead encourage others to retain a focus on their immediate work content.

- Increase your chances of success by making commitment contracts to reach your goals. Write them down and highlight your intended start date. To provide even more focus, consider using a more radical solution and visit stickk.com to create a commitment contract with some serious consequences.

- Embrace personal responsibility for adding value to the organisation by always considering the total cost implications and the impact on your end users.

- Introduce action learning sets across your department. Get colleagues to work in small groups to tackle important issues and learn from their experience by exploring and adapting accepted practices.

18

▲ Publicly parade your support for colleagues who are results focused. Concentrate your energies on those people who habitually qualify their requests for assistance with well-defined action plans and who are able to express their desired outcomes clearly.

Inspiration

✛ Take flight. In many cases action is cheaper than planning. The Wright brothers had a tiny budget with which to develop their plane, yet still managed to beat other large corporations investing heavily in manned flight. They undertook hundreds of test flights and made small tweaks to each version they tested. In doing so they failed fastest and learned quickest.[287]

✛ Buy the book. Get hold of a pristine copy of *How to Be F*cking Awesome* by Dan Meredith and find loads of brilliant ways to take action, achieve what you want and avoid what you don't want.[288]

✛ Aim to deliver tiny results. Small incremental improvements can make a huge difference. The British Cycling team was transformed by Dave Brailsford, who focused on securing 1 per cent marginal improvements in everything the team did. He demonstrated that each small gain would add up to remarkable improvements by searching for 1 per cent improvements in areas overlooked by everyone else. Within three years, the team had won the Tour de France and 70 per cent of the Olympic cycling gold medals.[289]

✛ Read Jim Loehr and Tony Schwartz' article 'The Making of a Corporate Athlete' and explore the benefits of building in planned recovery time after periods of prolonged stretch.[290]

 ## Related work skills

Commercial Thinking (2), Commitment to Change and Adaptation (3), Direction and Purpose (6), Effective Planning and Organisation (7), Motivation to Succeed (12), Ownership of Self-Development (13), Positive Decisions (15), Teamwork and Collaboration (20).

Results through Action

18

KEY 19

Specialist Knowledge and Ability

Specialist Knowledge and Ability

People who develop specialist knowledge and abilities adopt a proactive approach to acquiring the skills and professional understanding required for their defined area of work. They demonstrate an awareness of the knowledge and standards relevant to their role and the value these bring. Great at facilitating opportunities for professional learning, they are likely to convey a passion and enthusiasm for their subject area. They are able to extend their subject knowledge through professional networking and learning from others both inside and outside the organisation. By focusing on vocationally relevant concerns, these single-minded individuals may have the capacity to share expertise with others and translate their knowledge into practical applications.

 ## Ideas for personal development

> *When you find an idea that you just can't stop thinking about, that's probably a good one to pursue.*
>
> **Josh James**

Tool

- Use Jerry Seinfeld's 'Don't break the chain' model to help deal with procrastination and increase productivity in your chosen field. Select a task and put a large, visible X on your calendar for every day you work on it. The string of unbroken X's will serve as an incentive to keep going. iPhone apps such as Streaks and Rituals follow the same principle.

19

Techniques

▲ Start by believing that becoming an expert in your field is achievable. Seek to extend your personal capability in your existing role beyond the level ordinarily expected.

▲ Find your passion. Pay close attention to what it is you do differently to everyone else. In situations where you are using your own unique strengths, you will always stand out from the crowd. Identify what you love doing and try to do more of it, or integrate parts into your job if possible. If you can't discover your passion, get hold of a copy of *The Element* by Ken Robinson and read it.[291]

▲ Acknowledge and adhere to all the relevant professional standards for your role.

▲ Recognise that practice doesn't always make perfect – it makes permanent. Doing something repetitively means you may plateau, so get some external input through feedback and stretch your boundaries.

▲ Subscribe and engage with any occupationally relevant groups on social media and access vocationally targeted virtual environments.

▲ Actively facilitate opportunities for professional learning. Record all your continuing professional development and involve your line manager in your plans.

Inspiration

✦ Put your best foot forward. If you are just setting out on your journey of specialist enquiry, fuel up by reading *Novice to Expert* by Steve Scott.[292] This easy and informative introduction to expanding your existing knowledge will help you to immerse yourself in your chosen area of interest and learn new skills.

✦ Cultivate an appetite for personal development and prioritise vocationally relevant concerns. Watch Josh Kaufman's TEDx Talk on 'The First 20 Hours – How to Learn Anything'.[293]

19

+ Focus on one subject or discipline at a time. Commit to it. Charles M. Schulz drew the *Peanuts* comic strip for fifty years. He created nearly 18,000 Charlie Brown strips during his lifetime.

⚙ Ideas for delivering results

> *You are more likely to acquire power by narrowing your focus and applying your energies, like the sun's rays, to a limited range of activities in a small number of domains.*
>
> **Jeffrey Pfeffe**

Tools

- Don't have time to keep up to date with developments in your field? Test the free trial of blinkist.com, which lets you enjoy bite-sized insights in audio or text from thousands of non-fiction books in fifteen minutes or less.

- Check out skillshare.com, which is aimed at connecting experts in any domain with people interested in learning about them.

- Use Twitter, Facebook and LinkedIn to interact with others in your field. Write guest blogs and articles for trade magazines and professional journals – bolster your authority status in your discipline.

Techniques

- Define the scope of your specialist area and make sure you are able to explain how it contributes to your organisational objectives.

- Join a professionally recognised association for your field. Attend regional meetings and get involved.

19

- Avoid jargon. It pushes people away. Make complicated topics easy to understand. Explain what you do and why simply.

- Identify simple ways to anticipate future occupational requirements. Talk to your customers and colleagues about their needs and experiences.

- You may sometimes need to get the badge. Frustratingly for some, formal qualifications still denote 'true expert' status in certain roles. Investigate the most transferable skills for your subject area and explore what support is available in these fields.

- Be curious. People who extend their specialist knowledge are curious about their discipline and recognise the limitations of their own understanding.

- Spread the word. Using a variety of teaching methods will increase the understandability of your subject with most groups, helping you to come across as more credible and informed.

- Share widely. Not only will more people appreciate why they need you around, but it will also build trust in you. Deliver high level, respected advice to others based on your thorough understanding of your subject area.

- Identify local experts, ask for assistance and identify opportunities for shared learning.

- List the five eminent thinkers in your field. Take each specialist, one at a time, and source their most important contributions. Pick two or three of these and summarise their work on a single page using a mind-map or flash words. Connect each thinker.

- Create your own signature model or package. Develop a unique way of doing something to solve an existing problem, package the idea, then talk to an intellectual property lawyer to find out whether or not your idea can be protected.

- Hone your ability to communicate well. Specialist knowledge is only valuable if people know it exists and can understand the content.

- Get involved with podcasting, radio interviews and other media postings.

- Reassure yourself that it is okay to swim in a pond full of generalists. Lots of success, credibility and kudos can be achieved from being acknowledged as a subject expert.

- Micro-specialise – consider specialising within your specialism. Focusing your efforts on a defined group or niche market will also make personal branding much easier.

Inspiration

- Get yourself a copy of *Mastery* by Robert Greene.[294] Discover proven ways to immerse yourself in a given field of study, stay true to your preferences and actualise your long-term potential – no matter how unconventional your interests may seem to others. Once you've finished reading this book, pick up *Peak: Secrets from the New Science of Expertise* by Anders Ericsson and Robert Pool and find out how to get even better at the things you are already good at.[295]

- Never stop. While specialist knowledge grows incrementally and expertise is a relative term, it has been estimated by Malcolm Gladwell that it takes 10,000 hours to truly master a subject or skill.[296] Recent research suggests this is especially true in fields with stable structures, such as tennis and chess, where the rules rarely change.[297]

19

✈ Ideas for long-term gain

> … here is the prime condition of success, the great secret:
> concentrate your energy, thought, and capital exclusively upon
> the business in which you are engaged. Having begun in one
> line, resolve to fight it out on that line, to lead in it; adopt every
> improvement, have the best machinery, and know the most
> about it.
>
> **Andrew Carnegie**

Tool

▪ Pop over to docs-engine.com for a wide range of specialist
documents and published articles. If you are conducting
research, investigating a subject or preparing a report, this
search engine can provide helpful links to resources and articles
which can then be accessed or downloaded.

Techniques

▲ Write a short book about a defined problem, outlining your
suggested solution. Keep it simple and self-publish it.

▲ Provide seminars, presentations and speeches to people who
know little about your subject – engage with others and
reposition your messages.

▲ Seek out a credible mentor and at the same time make yourself
available to your less experienced colleagues.

▲ Acknowledge the value that generalist knowledge offers to the
organisation. Actively involve people with broad-based skills in
your project work where appropriate.

▲ Organise and manage an informal professional alliance of like-
minded people in your area of specialism and invite others in
your field to contribute to it.

19

- Apply deliberate practice techniques to improve your skills at a higher level.[298] Continually challenge yourself by starting with a clear goal, splitting it into sub-goals, keeping track of progress, getting feedback and avoiding distractions.

- Learn by training those around you. Teaching others has been shown to improve your own mental performance.[299] Identify emerging trends in your field, research into them and then provide training sessions to others in your team.

- Develop a reputation for being a generous expert – someone who shares specialist knowledge and insight freely and without hesitation. Become an advocate and an educator for your end users.

Inspiration

- Don't be too pleased with what you already know. Be more aware of how unaware you actually are. Monitor any inclination to becoming rather proud of your ever growing level of expertise. Visit youarenotsosmart.com and read David McRaney's celebration of self-delusion blog or pick up a copy of his book, *You Are Not So Smart*.[300] Discover how your own brilliant brain can often go wrong, and pick up some surprising techniques to put it right.

Related work skills

Commercial Thinking (2), Creativity and Innovation (5), Effective Planning and Organisation (7), Focus on Developing Others (9), Motivation to Succeed (12), Ownership of Self-Development (13), Professional Ethics and Social Responsibility (16), Use of Information and Data (21).

19

KEY 20

Teamwork and Collaboration

Teamwork and Collaboration

People who work well in teams and collaborate effectively with others participate through a spirit of cooperation and commitment to achieve shared goals. They recognise and accept complementary roles and acknowledge the advantages of a variance of approach. They are more disposed to share their ideas and support and have a capacity for building on the suggestions of those around them. They are able to operate with confidence in virtual teams, project groups and self-directed workgroups. These adaptable individuals involve others through open consultation and are inclined to develop strong work relationships. They encourage the use of shared problem solving along with mutual accountability to drive team unity. By acting as a custodian of the group, they are likely to contribute to the development of a clear team identity.

 ## Ideas for personal development

> *Individual commitment to a group effort – that is what makes a team work, a company work, a society work, a civilization work.*
>
> **Vince Lombardi**

Tools

- Encourage team members to be open with each other from the outset. Try using a personal histories exercise in the first few weeks to encourage unguarded conversations and build rapport.

- Buy spaghetti and build better teams. Discover how a popular pasta-based team building exercise can provide powerful messages about collaborative effort and experimentation by watching Tom Wujec's TED Talk 'Build a Tower, Build a Team'.[301]

- Look at an old model in a new light. Studies confirm that Bruce Tuckman's stages of group development model still applies to many teams as they go through forming, storming, norming, performing and adjourning during their lifecycle.[302] Explore techniques to move smoothly through each of the five stages by recognising that extending opportunities for collaboration and integrative decision making may help with the management of these transitions.

Techniques

- If you are joining a new team or starting one from scratch, be conscious of putting too many strangers together as it can make people reluctant to share their knowledge. Always select the right individuals, but if possible build on heritage relationships and include a few people who already have some kind of connection to help the group gel.

- Superglue new teams together. Get them to engage in unusual, challenging and exciting activities which require working together to achieve a common goal. Get people involved in novel situations to accelerate levels of trust and help the team to bond more quickly.

- All point in the same direction. While a leader's role is to drive the adoption of a common goal, everyone can contribute towards this intention. Create a unifying sense of identity by getting every single person in the team involved in crafting a powerful one- or two-sentence statement about what the team is about.

- Build trust. There has to be confidence across all team members that their peers' intentions are good and there is no need to be protective around the group. People trust others who they believe are looking out for their best intentions. Be reliable. Be truthful.

- Be clear about who does what, but also support effective working relationships by actively promoting role variance and difference instead of conformity and convergence.

- Tolerate variance in terms of levels of affiliation. Some people are more comfortable with their own company than others, so don't force them to change. However, this doesn't prevent them from engaging in team discussions and events and collaborating on key tasks.

Inspiration

- Small is beautiful. Although no defined size works best for effective teams, the accepted wisdom remains that the fewer the numbers involved, the greater the chance of collaboration. Management guru Tom Peters notes how 'big groups tend to reinvent the wheel', while smaller groups improvise.[303]

⚙️ Ideas for delivering results

> *Strength lies in differences, not in similarities.*
>
> **Stephen Covey**

Tools

- Create generative relationships using the STAR technique. Work together effectively by respecting: Separateness (different perspectives), Tuning (talking and listening), Action opportunities and the Reason to work together.

20

- Download the Slack app to use as a handy collaboration tool. It is ideal for interdepartmental communications, helping people to interact, share updates and keep informed on what is going on. Other options include Google Docs, Samepage and Yammer. Track team progress on short- and long-term goals using Asana.

- Give team role inventories a wide berth during times of transition. While it may be convenient to assign people to generic team types, the speed of change and the complexity of today's work situation demands a more fluid and adaptive approach to understanding evolving capabilities in the workplace.

- Avoid groupthink.[304] Minimise the possibility that evolved teams defer to each other and unintentionally suppress individual ideas by using the stepladder technique – a simple way to encourage all members to freely contribute before being influenced by anyone else. Stepladder decision making has also been found to significantly improve the overall quality of decisions made.[305]

- Get chatty. Try out one of the latest digital solutions for developing team performance using a chatbot app such as Saberr's CoachBot, which provides personalised bite-sized coaching – thereby enabling teams to access support at a time which suits them.

- Read up on the Drexler/Sibbet team performance model.[306] This handy visual framework outlines the seven stages required for both creating and sustaining effective teams and can be used to develop a common language for supporting a team-based culture.

Techniques

- Get it together. Be interested in, and committed to, the contributions and ideas of others. Make everyone aware of how they personally contribute and hold each person accountable for their actions. Incorporate team-based problem solving into your meetings. Invite peers to share issues they are facing and ask for constructive ideas to solve them. Encourage open and frequent communication by all and foster an environment where any conflict can be freely aired and managed.

▲ Share your online calendars. Provide access to everyone's diary and movements to ensure the whole team are on the same page and appreciate the different demands people face.

▲ Individual talents may be less important to team effectiveness than group communication patterns, so maximise opportunities for face-to-face transactions. New studies suggest that as much as 35 per cent of a team's performance may be explained by tallying the number of face-to-face exchanges between members.[307] The way individuals communicate with each other has also been found to be more important than what they communicate.

▲ Be ruthless. Great teams provide ruthless encouragement to each other. Recognise team efforts and celebrate successes.

▲ Promote a creative atmosphere across your team. Once ways of working are established, apply as few rules as possible. Define the tasks, then provide latitude in terms of how they are achieved. Be comfortable with role clarity and task ambiguity. Regard any mistakes as part of the learning process.

▲ Pilot the use of a dedicated social networking page for team members to interact in and out of work. Ensure open access to all the team and review its effectiveness after three months.

▲ Effective teams regularly evaluate their own performance. Try asking these six killer questions: what is the purpose of your team? Who are the key stakeholders? What are the current priorities? How do you know the team is performing well? What are your main strengths? How do you motivate a diverse group of people?

▲ Revisit team performance measures. Are they clear and easy to follow? Are they reliable? Most importantly, is there equal access across the team to all the required information?

▲ Run a bespoke team development session using a professional facilitator to introduce relevant experiential exercises away from the work environment.

20

🔺 Hold productive meetings – making them short and sweet. Consider using an impartial observer to oversee the process and make sure you are on track with the tasks. Allow team members to lead meetings when their area of responsibility is discussed. Invite everyone to share issues they are facing and ask for constructive ideas to solve them.

Inspiration

✦ Minute by minute. Follow the advice given by Ken Blanchard, co-author of *The One Minute Manager*, and always put essence before form to build collaboration at work.[308] Essence is about hearts and values ('Tell me about yourself ...', 'What is important to you?'). Form is about how you are going to do it (who will do what, how to allocate tasks). Both are vital; however, one should come before the other.

✦ Learn from geese. Download a copy of 'Lessons from Geese' by Angeles Arrien and apply these principles to how you respond when working in your own team.[309]

✦ Watch Jim Tamm's TEDx Talk on 'Cultivating Collaboration' and discover the single most powerful way to increase collaborative effort across any team.[310]

✦ Build cohesion by involving your team at the planning stages of any anticipated change. Encourage the use of non-competitive language. Strengthen relationships by asking everyone to watch Joe Gebbia's TED Talk on 'How Airbnb Designs for Trust'.[311]

Teamwork and Collaboration

20

✈ Ideas for long-term gain

> *None of us is as smart as all of us.*
>
> **Ken Blanchard**

Tools

- Encourage everyone to complete the Margerison–McCann Team Management Profile.[312] Not only will it confirm evolving team preferences and identify opportunities to build productivity, but it will also help each person to understand the implications of their work orientations and how they can interact to build a high performing, high energy team.

- Paint your own canvas. Nip over to theteamcanvas.com and grab a copy of *Team Canvas* by Alex Ivanov and Mitya Voloshchuk. Discover a powerful free tool for initiating team discussions and maintaining your desired culture and values.

- Make individual progress available to the whole team. Research the PPP process used by Skype and eBay. Use this to summarise and share how everyone is doing by capturing feedback on Progress, Plans and Problems.

Techniques

- Identify tangible actions you can take to encourage people to be more open about mistakes and vulnerabilities, engage in unguarded debate, explore ideas and commit to plans.

- Allow team members to solve big issues. Give them a say when recruiting new members. Rely on the knowledge and experience of your colleagues when it comes to decision making and give them the power to influence the things they will be affected by.

20

▲ Value expertise but keep an eye on the experts. Harvard research suggests that the greater the proportion of experts on a team, the more likely it is to disintegrate into non-productive conflict or stalemate.[313]

Inspiration

✦ Back to black. Banish the ego to strengthen team spirit. Take the lead from the New Zealand All Blacks and bring everyone together to share a common task at certain times. Before leaving the dressing room at the end of every game, every single All Black player has to stop and tidy up after themselves. Each player 'sweeps the sheds', regardless of their position or role.

✦ Understand why teams fail. Get hold of a copy of *The Five Dysfunctions of a Team* by Patrick Lencioni, and use his questionnaire to assess the current effectiveness of your workgroup by inviting contributions from your whole team.[314]

✦ Mange better teams by looking into the 'rule of five'. Trello founder Joel Spolsky asks all his employees for feedback on only five items, helping them to prioritise their workloads and accomplish more through the creation of personal boundaries.

✦ Break down departmental walls. Focus on improving work structures to help you expand and grow more easily. If you operate in a large, complex environment, investigate how IBM, Skyscanner, ING and Spotify have organised their work processes. Consider tailoring specific agile project management principles to your own culture to help transform your working groups into flexible, self-managed cross-functional 'squads' and 'tribes'.

 Related work skills

Ability to Influence (1), Constructive Communication (4), Creativity and Innovation (5), Direction and Purpose (6), Focus on Developing Others (9), Interpersonal Awareness and Diplomacy (10), People Management and Leadership Potential (14), Results through Action (18).

KEY 21
Use of Information and Data

Use of Information and Data

People who excel at using information and data effectively gather material in a systematic way to establish facts and principles. They are able to access, explore, analyse and interpret from a wide range of reliable data sources. Capable of testing assumptions against evidence, they can identify trends and patterns and identify errors and inconsistencies. These detail-conscious individuals make rational judgements based on a thorough assessment of available information and are able to organise content to make it more coherent and clear. They excel at filtering out unnecessary and redundant elements. Typically, they are likely to promote the adoption of emerging digital technologies for appropriate tasks and will have a capacity for disseminating information, ensuring the material provided is both accurate and relevant to others.

 ## Ideas for personal development

> Data beats emotions.
>
> **Sean Rad**

Tools

- Use the Pocket app to save a text-only version of all those interesting articles and great web pages you don't have time to read right now.

■ Swipe your way to a clearer inbox. Download the Unroll.Me app to instantly see a list of all your subscription emails. Unsubscribe easily from whatever you don't want and manage those you do.

Techniques

▲ Get excited – information can be cool. Recognise that it provides structure to randomness, helps to reduce uncertainty, has a role in making selections, helps you to recognise the importance of probability and is the basis for rational decisions.

▲ Differentiate between data and information. Regard data as the raw material which needs to be processed before it becomes useful, while information is derived from this process and can be used to inform decisions.

▲ Improve your attention span and minimise any errors when analysing data. Reduce distractions by performing high concentration tasks away from phones and emails. Turn off email alerts. Spend five minutes unsubscribing from unwanted mailing lists by searching for the word 'unsubscribe' in your inbox to help you target unwanted emails. Cluster similar tasks together. Respond to emails at designated times during the day.

▲ Focus first on the source and credibility of any data received, and encourage others to do the same. Dig into the credibility of the source material. Ask yourself: who said this? What is their experience? What was their motivation at the time?

▲ Review the amount of information you try to retain in your head at the same time. Externalise data and write it down. Doing so prevents mental lethargy and ensures accuracy of recall. Annotate your information with creation, review and archive dates.

▲ Get chunky. The human brain can only hold a limited number of pieces of information in its working memory at once.[315] Create smaller chunks of information to help improve retention: 724845276 is less easily retrieved than 724 845 276.

▲ Gather and collate. Review any information you would like to present in terms of its accuracy and validity. Seek to identify patterns and trends. Edit the material and distil it into key points. Cluster similar items together – advantages, disadvantages, resources, people, hazards.

Inspiration

✦ Delve deeper into data. Read up on a little known clock maker called William Harrison, whose commitment to excellence in measurement transformed the way data is used today and improved the safety of every vessel at sea. Check out *Longitude* by Dava Sobel.[316]

⚙ Ideas for delivering results

> *Data becomes information when it's organised; information becomes knowledge when it is placed in actionable context. Without context, there is little value.*
>
> **Kent Greenes**

Tools

▪ Get organised. Apply the Five Hat Racks method (or LATCH technique) to manage your information. Organise it all by use of: Location (think London Underground map), Alphabet, Time (flowcharts, timelines), Category and Hierarchy.

▪ Go fishing. If you are struggling to draw out themes where there are a large number of possible causes, construct a large fishbone diagram using masking tape. The Ishikawa method is a great way to recognise cause-and-effect relationships.[317]

- Test your analytic skills by undertaking an accredited psychometric test approved by the British Psychological Society and compare your performance to other relevant norm groups.

Techniques

- Be a relationship person. Studies reveal that people who are effective at recognising relationships between sets of unrelated information perform better across a range of managerial tasks.[318]

- Facilitate an even spread of information contribution. People are more likely to share when they have a perceived higher status. To encourage lower status members to share their knowledge, their expertise needs to be specifically acknowledged by the wider group.

- Demonstrate to others the importance of valuing evidence over opinion. Encourage your peers to access and distribute information which they can demonstrate has been derived from a multitude of sources.

- Manage your attention by monitoring the number of tasks you try to undertake at the same time. While the majority of emails in the workplace are acknowledged within the first two minutes of their arrival, it can take up to twenty minutes for an employee to return to the same level of productivity they were achieving prior to this distraction. Rapid task-switching has also been associated with a temporary lowering of IQ.[319]

- Mix it up. Make more decisions based on an evaluation of all the appropriate data by accessing a good network of information sources. Apply a blend of quantitative and qualitative data and extend opportunities to accommodate a wide number of contributors when trying to understand a particular problem.

- Evaluate received information and reports by considering their format and structure. Consider if an initial summary of the key points is evident and whether overt benefits are included. Have alternative views or explanations been ignored? Was any jargon used without explanation? Is there an absence of visible and progressive stages which you can follow? Can you identify any glaring contradictions? Does a lack of relationship with previous statements exist? Is the sequence unclear or illogical? Have any basic assumptions not been questioned? Have any opinions been used as facts? Are any of the arguments presented as absolutes? Importantly, does the material relate to the outcomes desired?

▲ Get familiar with the General Data Protection Regulations (GDPR) and any requirements relating to Freedom of Information requests. Fully explore all the legal responsibilities relating to the transmission and storage of any information you hold.

▲ Practise explaining any processes in a step-by-step way. When required to share your material with others, create an accessible framework by applying focus, structure and action to it. Deliver the essence of the information quickly, break the argument into easy-to-follow stages and build some forward movement to it.

▲ Take responsibility for all your own information consumption. Question whether you are choosing to overload your mind with non-essential details. Encourage others around you to take personal responsibility for managing their information absorption and, in doing so, influencing their personal effectiveness.

▲ Debate your ideas to improve collective understanding. Invite diverse representatives from around the organisation. Structure your thoughts by moving through past, present and future to add focus and dynamism to your information.

Inspiration

✦ Read *The Organised Mind* by Daniel Levitin.[320]

✦ Develop an appetite. Watch J. P. Rangaswami's illuminating TED Talk 'Information Is Food' to learn how data can be regarded as nourishment for the mind in the same way that food is nourishment for the body.[321]

21

- Master the fundamentals. Get into data science to enhance your career. Pick up practical advice on developing visualisation, modelling, preparation, presentation and communication techniques in *Confident Data Skills* by Kirill Eremenko.[322] Discover how real-world data skills are being applied at Netflix, LinkedIn, Goodreads, AlphaGo and Deep Blue.

- Stop the secrecy. When asked to make a group decision, the human inclination is to – instead of share vital information known only to themselves – repeat information everyone already knows. Google 'Stasser and Titus' and discover how to overcome one of the greatest blockages to information flow across your organisation.[323]

- Help others to take flight. At your next team meeting, explore the implications of the following quote attributed to Jan Carlzon, former CEO of Scandinavian Airlines System (SAS): 'An individual without information cannot take responsibility; an individual who is given information cannot help but take responsibility.' Consider what needs to be shared and how this can most effectively be achieved.

- Engage with a professional animator to represent complex ideas and information in a graphical format and use the images to support communication of key points to other stakeholders. To find out how simple diagrams can clarify your messages, watch David McCandless' TED Talk 'The Beauty of Data Visualization'.[324]

- Excel at the tell. Emulate honorary American Statistical Association member Florence Nightingale by making all your information accessible and interesting. As a pioneer of quantitative methods, she insisted on the creation of imaginative, colourful charts and diagrams to ensure her contentious data on military care mortality rates was both clear and indisputable.[325]

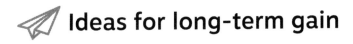 Ideas for long-term gain

> *Information is the oil of the 21st century, and analytics is the combustion engine.*
>
> **Peter Sondergaard**

Tools

▪ Know your information types. Use the 'Anthony triangle' to appreciate the three levels of decision making information available across your organisation.[326] Being able to differentiate between strategic, tactical and operational information sources will help you to plan objectives for the whole organisation, understand how resources can be best employed and ensure specific tasks are carried out as planned.

▪ Always test the robustness of any conclusions reached. Once you have captured sufficient information, try using thought experiments to examine each situation more fully. Employ methodology from gaming theory such as 'beetle in a box'. Alternatively, practise a more philosophical approach by introducing Schrödinger's cat paradox to provoke deeper thinking.

Techniques

▲ Optimise the use of technology to support an integrated approach to organisational information flow, including web content management, document management, records management, digital asset management and learning management.

- Invest in training and development to increase analytical capability. Studies reveal that unstructured organic training in this area is often more effective than formal courses which focus more on the why rather than the how.[327] Concentrate efforts on peer-to-peer work and mentoring rather than software and mechanical skills for the greatest long-term gain.

- Eradicate the mystique surrounding MIS (Management Information Systems). Share how your MIS is used to translate data into practical advantage. Make simple analogies to describe your system – like a database with some added intelligence. Many MIS systems follow a set of rules and algorithms which govern how the data is used, wrapped up in a user interface to present different types of data on demand.

- Gravitate towards excellence. Analytical acumen has been found to be highest among research and development teams, senior managers and Generation X's.[328] Surround yourself with talented people and replicate their approaches.

- Remember the higher up the mountain you climb, the thinner the air. If presenting a proposal or information pack to members of your most senior team, it is likely that your directors will want key summaries and overviews, not all the detail. You will have been empowered to come up with recommendations, not a complete review of the methodology. The higher the mountain, the thinner the air; the thinner the air, the greater the need to concentrate.

Inspiration

- Love your data. Less than 1 per cent of businesses say that analytics will not be important to their business in five years' time. Read *Winning with Data* by Tomasz Tunguz and Frank Bien and learn how to empower your people.[329] Encourage others to appreciate well-founded information based on reasoned enquiry.

- It's a hoot! Create a free Hootsuite account to manage all of your organisational social media postings in one place. Buffer and TweetDeck provide similar zero-cost alternatives.

✦ Use your sixth sense. If tasked with resolving large technical issues on a regular basis, always investigate the possible root causes first. Take corrective action to fix the issue, but also look around the problem to fix the underlying causes on a permanent basis. Six Sigma's DMAIC (Define, Measure, Analyse, Improve, Control) is one data driven improvement cycle used for analysing and improving business processes.[330]

 # Related work skills

Commercial Thinking (2), Effective Planning and Organisation (7), Enthusiasm for Customer Service (8), Intuitive Thought (11), Positive Decisions (15), Results through Action (18), Specialist Knowledge and Ability (19).

Use of Information and Data

21

Summary

Reflecting the changing world of work

The future belongs to those who learn more skills and combine them in creative ways.

Robert Greene

Traditional methods of managing performance are coming under increasing scrutiny. In the workplace there is a movement away from routine, annualised performance management systems in favour of ongoing feedback which can be delivered throughout the year. Larger companies such as Google, Deloitte and Accenture have recognised that bureaucratic, process driven staff appraisals often fail to provide the flexibility to deal with rapid change and have abandoned them in favour of a more fluid, open ended approach. The adoption of a continuous performance management approach relies on the introduction of shorter-term objectives linked to individual task requirements. This encourages more frequent conversations between manager and employee to discuss performance expectations on a project-by-project basis, providing an ideal platform for the introduction of short, self-managed approaches to professional development at the point of need.

Many performance management systems were introduced alongside competency frameworks back in the early 1980s. While the original driver for many of these frameworks was to define the behavioural expectations required at a job level, they rarely succeed in accommodating the complexity of evolving job requirements.[331] The competency model was based on an old myth that the 'ideal employee' could actually be found. It suggested that it was possible to define a set of standards required for effective performance and that this 'magic formula for success' could be captured, articulated and shared in order to create some kind of blueprint for superior performance. The implication was that employees somehow needed 'fixing' to perform at their best. Just like Rocky Balboa, people had 'gaps' – weaknesses which needed to be addressed before they could be rated as 'competent'. Frequently, these frameworks were created to help people to improve in areas in which they were naturally less effective.

However, recent studies have demonstrated that organisations are far more likely to deliver effective results by bolstering the strengths and talents of each person, instead of trying to transform their people into 'well-rounded individuals'.[332] This is the philosophy adopted by Facebook's vice president of people, Lori Goler, who made it her mission to make the big daddy of the social media world into what she termed a 'strengths-based' organisation. It looks like her approach is paying dividends because Facebook is now regularly cited as one of the best places to work in the United States today.

Competency frameworks are, by nature, evaluative. They provide an orderly structure to help assess performance in a consistent way – a way thought to be linked (although rarely proven) to success in role. Conversely, *Upskill* focuses solely on outcomes. By flipping the framework, the material in this handbook concentrates on what needs to happen to make a difference, by emphasising the 'so what?' factor. This is an approach which doesn't attempt to anticipate the requirements of a given role, but instead presents a range of practical ideas to extend performance based on the evolving needs of any particular task. Ultimately, of course, there is no 'magic bullet' or single solution to the evolving challenge of individual skills development, although it is hoped that the introduction of some of the high leverage suggestions contained in this book may help to encourage a more adaptive approach to personal and professional development – delivering a proven range of individualised learning options for anyone interested in developing the skills which are in greatest demand today.

Whichever mixture of tools and techniques you choose to apply in your quest to upskill, I wish you continued success.

Notes

Introduction

1   J. Heckman and T. D. Kautz, Hard Evidence on Soft Skills. *Labour Economics*, 19(4) (2012), 451–464.
2   UK Commission for Employment and Skills, *EmployerSkills Survey 2015: UK Report*. London: UKCES, 2015. Available at: https://www.gov.uk/government/publications/ukces-employer-skills-survey-2015-uk-report.
3   K. Davidson, Employers Find 'Soft Skills' Like Critical Thinking in Short Supply. *Wall Street Journal*, 30 August 2016. Available at: https://www.wsj.com/articles/employers-find-soft-skills-like-critical-thinking-in-short-supply-1472549400.
4   The Adaptive Skills Project (2006–2016) was an online survey conducted by Performance Talks Ltd/Endor Learn & Develop to investigate the adaptive skills most prized by employers. Feedback was received from occupational sectors including manufacturing, digital technologies, media and creative services, logistics, service industries, retail, food and drinks, engineering, plastics and polymers, agriculture, local government, education, voluntary services, nursing, healthcare, banking and insurance. Additional technical assistance was received from the Design Enterprise Centre at the University of Hull.
5   See https://www.kent.ac.uk/economics/documents/research/papers/2016/1612.pdf and https://www.youthemployment.org.uk/dev/wp-content/uploads/2017/07/Youth-Employment-UK-Employability-Review-June-2017.pdf.
6   Davidson, Employers Find 'Soft Skills' Like Critical Thinking in Short Supply.
7   World Economic Forum, *The Future of Jobs: Employment, Skills and Workforce Strategy for the Fourth Industrial Revolution* (Geneva: World Economic Forum, 2016). Available at: http://www3.weforum.org/docs/WEF_Future_of_Jobs.pdf.
8   B. Palmer, What Job Skills Will You Need in 2020? PCMA, 18 June 2018. Available at: https://www.pcma.org/what-job-skills-will-you-need-in-2020/.
9   W. Scott-Jackson, S. Owens, M. Saldana, L. Charles, M. Green, P. Woodman and L. Plas, *Learning to Lead: The Digital Potential* (London: Chartered Management Institute, 2015). Available at: https://www.managers.org.uk/~/media/Files/PDF/Digital-Learning/Learning_to_Lead-The_Digital_Potential.pdf.

Key 1

10   T. E. Barry, The Development of the Hierarchy of Effects: An Historical Perspective. *Current Issues and Research in Advertising*, 10(1–2) (1987), 251–295.
11   P. Y. Martin, J. Laing, R. Martin and M. Mitchell, Caffeine, Cognition, and Persuasion: Evidence for Caffeine Increasing the Systematic Processing of Persuasive Messages. *Journal of Applied Social Psychology*, 35 (2005), 160–182.
12   See https://rainmaker.fm/audio/lede/use-persuasive-words.
13   B. Schwartz, *The Paradox of Choice: Why More is Less*. New York: Harper Perennial, 2005.
14   E. Langer, A. Blank and B. Chanowitz, The Mindlessness of Ostensibly Thoughtful Action: The Role of 'Placebic' Information in Interpersonal Interaction. *Journal of Personality and Social Psychology*, 36(6) (1978), 635–642.

15 C. Handy, *Understanding Organizations*, 4th edn. Harmondsworth: Penguin, 1993, p. 387.

16 M. Feinberg and R. Willer, From Gulf to Bridge: When Do Moral Arguments Facilitate Political Influence? *Personality and Social Psychology Bulletin*, 41(12) (2015), 1665–1681.

17 R. Garner, Post-it® Note Persuasion: A Sticky Influence. *Journal of Consumer Psychology*, 15(3) (2005), 230–237.

18 S. M. Smith and D. R. Shaffer, Celerity and Cajolery: Rapid Speech May Promote or Inhibit Persuasion Through Its Impact on Message Elaboration. *Personality and Social Psychology Bulletin*, 17 (1991), 663–669.

19 D. Carnegie, *How to Win Friends and Influence People*. New York: Simon & Schuster, 1981 [1936].

20 See https://www.ted.com/talks/casey_brown_know_your_worth_and_then_ask_for_it.

21 P. Raghubir and A. Valenzuela, Center-of-Inattention: Position Biases in Decision-Making. *Organisational Behaviour and Human Decision Processes*, 99(1) (2006), 66–80.

22 See https://www.youtube.com/watch?v=ydchCy5WF_I.

23 N. Goldstein, S. J. Martin and R. B. Cialdini, *Yes! 60 Secrets from the Science of Persuasion*. London: Profile Books, 2017.

24 K. Patterson, J. Grenny, D. Maxfield, R. McMillan and A. Switzler, *Influencer: The Power to Change Anything*, 1st edn. New York: McGraw-Hill, 2007.

25 S. Benton, C. van Erkom Schurink and D. Desson, *An Overview of the Development, Validity and Reliability of the English Version 3.0 of the Insights Discovery Evaluator*. London: University of Westminster, 2008.

26 See https://www.kornferry.com/institute/the-four-stages-of-contribution.

27 C. Heath and D. Heath, *Made to Stick: Why Some Ideas Survive and Others Die*. New York: Random House, 2008.

28 G. Bohner, S. Einwiller, H. P. Erb and F. Siebler, When Small Means Comfortable: Relations Between Product Attributes in Two-Sided Advertising. *Journal of Consumer Psychology*, 13 (2003), 454–463.

29 J. Xie, S. Sreenivasan, G. Korniss, W. Zhang, C. Lim and B. K. Szymanski, Social Consensus through the Influence of Committed Minorities. *Physical Review E*, 84 (2011), 011130. doi:10.1103/PhysRevE.84.011130.

30 R. Fisher and W. Ury, *Getting to Yes: Negotiating an Agreement Without Giving In*, 2nd edn. New York: Houghton Mifflin, 1991.

31 J. Berger, *Invisible Influence: The Hidden Forces That Shape Behaviour*. New York: Simon & Schuster, 2016.

Key 2

32 K. Ohmae, *The Mind of the Strategist: The Art of Japanese Business*. New York: McGraw-Hill, 1991.

33 K. L. Shandrow, Deepak Chopra's 7 Tips for Business Success. *Entrepreneur Europe*, 8 September 2016. Available at: https://www.entrepreneur.com/article/282057.

34 D. Sola and J. Couturier, *How to Think Strategically*. London: Financial Times Publishing, 2013.

35 S. Godin, *The Dip: A Little Book That Teaches You When to Quit (and When to Stick)*. London: Penguin, 2007.

36 R. H. Waterman, T. J. Peters and J. R. Phillips, Structure Is Not Organization. *Business Horizons*, 23(3) (1980), 14–26.

37 A. G. Lafley and R. L. Martin, *Playing to Win: How Strategy Really Works*. Boston, MA: Harvard Business Review Press, 2013.

38 J. Collins, *Good to Great: Why Some Companies Make the Leap – and Others Don't*. London: Random House Business, 2001.

39 Y. Moon, *Different: Escaping the Competitive Herd*. New York: Crown Business, 2011.

Key 3

40 S. Covey, *The Seven Habits of Highly Effective People*. New York: Simon & Schuster, 1992.

41 L. Smith, *The Moment: Wild, Poignant, Life-Changing Stories from 125 Writers and Artists Famous and Obscure*. New York: HarperCollins, 2012.

42 A. Deutschman, *Change or Die: The Three Keys to Change at Work and in Life*. New York: Harper Business, 2007.

43 J. B. Rotter, Generalized Expectancies for Internal Versus External Control of Reinforcement. *Psychological Monographs: General & Applied*, 80(1) (1966), 1–28.

44 S. Glucksberg, The Influence of Strength of Drive on Functional Fixedness and Perceptual Recognition. *Journal of Experimental Psychology*, 63(1) (1962), 36–41.

45 J. Silveira, Incubation: The Effect of Interruption Timing and Length on Problem Solution and Quality of Problem Processing. Unpublished doctoral dissertation, University of Oregon, 1971.

46 D. Rock, SCARF: A Brain-Based Model for Collaborating with and Influencing Others. *NeuroLeadership Journal*, 1 (2008), 78–87.

47 E. Kübler-Ross, *On Death and Dying*. New York: Macmillan, 1969.

48 J. Acuff, *Finish: Give Yourself the Gift of Done*. London: Penguin, 2017.

49 M. McKeown, *Adaptability: The Art of Winning in an Age of Uncertainty*. London: Kogan Page, 2012.

50 E. Tolle, *A New Earth: Awakening to Your Life's Purpose*. London: Penguin, 2009, p. 19.

51 See https://www.youtube.com/watch?v=lC25e-htHZo.

52 C. Heath and D. Heath, *Switch: How to Change Things When Change is Hard*. New York: Random House, 2011.

53 J. P. Kotter, *Leading Change*. New York: Harvard Business, 2002.

54 M. Jacka and P. Keller, *Business Process Mapping: Improving Customer Satisfaction*. Hoboken, NJ: John Wiley & Sons, 2009.

55 M. H. Shah, An Application of ADKAR Change Model for the Change Management Competencies of School Heads in Pakistan. *Journal of Managerial Sciences*, 8(1) (2014), 77–95.

56 G. Hamel, *What Matters Now: How to Win in a World of Relentless Change, Ferocious Competition, and Unstoppable Innovation*. San Francisco, CA: Jossey-Bass, 2012.

57 C. Duhigg, *The Power of Habit: Why We Do What We Do, and How to Change*. New York: Random House, 2013.

Key 4

58 N. Kline, *Time to Think: Listening to Ignite the Human Mind*. London: Hachette UK, 1999.

59 M. P. Nichols, *The Lost Art of Listening: How Learning to Listen Can Improve Relationships*. New York: Guilford Press, 2009.

60   A. Palmer, *The Art of Asking: How I Learned to Stop Worrying and Let People Help*. London: Piatkus, 2014.

61   See https://www.ted.com/talks/adam_galinsky_how_to_speak_up_for_ yourself.

62   F. Schulz von Thun, *Miteinander reden: Störungen und Klärungen. Psychologie der zwischenmenschlichen Kommunikation*. Rowohlt: Reinbek, 1981.

63   A. Aron, E. Melinat, E. N. Aron, R. D. Vallone and R. J. Bator, The Experimental Generation of Interpersonal Closeness: A Procedure and Some Preliminary Findings. *Personality and Social Psychology Bulletin*, 23 (1997), 363–377.

64   E. P. Leanse, Google and Apple Alum Says Using This Word Can Damage Your Credibility. *Business Insider*, 25 June 2015. Available at: http://www. businessinsider.com/former-google-exec-says-this-word-can-damage-your-credibility-2015-6?IR=T.

65   See https://www.youtube.com/watch?v=Ks-_Mh1QhMc.

66   H. F. Garcia, *The Power of Communication: Skills to Build Trust, Inspire Loyalty, and Lead Effectively*. Upper Saddle River, NJ: Pearson Education, 2012.

67   R. Dowis, *The Lost Art of the Great Speech: How to Write One – How to Deliver it*. New York: AMACOM, 2000.

68   D. F. Womack, A Review of Conflict Instruments in Organisational Settings. *Management Communication Quarterly*, 1(3) (1988), 437–445.

69   P. R. Madson, *Improve Wisdom: Don't Prepare, Just Show Up*. New York: Harmony-Bell Tower, 2005.

70   A. Alshamsi, F. Pianesi, B. Lepri, A. Pentland and I. Rahwan, Network Diversity and Affect Dynamics: The Role of Personality Traits. *PLOS ONE*, 11(4) (2016). Available at: http://journals.plos.org/plosone/article?id=10.1371/journal.pone.0152358.

Key 5

71   J. W. Young, *A Technique for Producing Ideas*. New York: McGraw Hill Professional, 2003.

72   J. Cameron, *The Artist's Way: A Spiritual Path to Higher Creativity*. New York: Penguin Putnam, 2016.

73   L. Huang, F. Gino and A. D. Galinsky, The Highest Form of Intelligence: Sarcasm Increases Creativity for Both Expressers and Recipients. *Organizational Behavior and Human Decision Processes*, 131 (2015), 162–177.

74   See https://www.ted.com/talks/elizabeth_gilbert_on_genius.

75   See https://www.ted.com/talks/ken_robinson_says_schools_kill_creativity.

76   M. H. Jones, S. D. West and D. B. Estell, The Mozart Effect: Arousal, Preference, and Spatial Performance. *Psychology of Aesthetics, Creativity, and the Arts*, S(1) (2006), 26–32.

77   See http://www.debonogroup.com/six_thinking_hats.php.

78   B. Eberle, *SCAMPER: Games for Imagination Development*. Austin, TX: Prufrock Press, 2008.

79   See https://www.ted.com/talks/marily_oppezzo_want_to_be_more_creative_ go_for_a_walk.

80   D. Oppenheimer, Hard-to-Read Fonts Promote Better Recall. *Harvard Business Review*, 90 (2012), 32–33.

81   H. Elrod, *The Miracle Morning: The 6 Habits That Will Transform Your Life Before 8am*. London: John Murray Learning, 2016.

82   D. M. Lipnicki and D. G. Byrne, Thinking On Your Back: Solving Anagrams Faster When Supine Than When Standing. *Cognitive Brain Research*, 24(3) (2005), 719–722.

83 R. Mehta, R. Zhu and A. Cheema, Is Noise Always Bad? Exploring the Effects of Ambient Noise on Creative Cognition. *Journal of Consumer Research*, 39(4) (2012), 784–799.

84 A. Grant, *Originals: How Non-Conformists Change the World*. London: Virgin Books, 2017, p. 109.

85 M. Zomorodi, *Bored and Brilliant: How Time Spent Doing Nothing Changes Everything*. New York: St Martin's Press, 2017.

86 See https://www.ted.com/talks/manoush_zomorodi_how_boredom_can_lead_to_your_most_brilliant_ideas.

87 T. Fowler, *The Elements of Deductive Logic: Designed Mainly for the Use of Junior Students in the Universities*, 3rd edn. Oxford: Clarendon Press, 1869, p. 163.

88 D. Kahneman, *Thinking, Fast and Slow*. London: Penguin, 2012.

89 D. Burkus, Decisions Might Be Better When Teams Don't Get Along. *Nature Human Behaviour*, 1 (2017), 0109. doi:10.1038/s41562-017-0109.

90 See https://www.ted.com/talks/linda_hill_how_to_manage_for_collective_creativity.

Key 6

91 D. Soman and A. Cheema, When Goals Are Counterproductive: The Effects of Violation of a Behavioural Goal on Subsequent Performance. *Journal of Consumer Research*, 31(1) (2004), 52–62.

92 V. E. Frankl, *Man's Search for Meaning*. Boston, MA: Beacon Press, 2006 [1946], p. 69.

93 See https://www.youtube.com/watch?v=6MBaFL7sCb8.

94 B. Burnett and D. Evans, *Designing Your Life: How to Build a Well-Lived, Joyful Life*. New York: Knopf Doubleday, 2017.

95 Carnegie, *How to Win Friends and Influence People*, p. 236.

96 T. M. Amabile and S. J. Kramer, The Power of Small Wins. *Harvard Business Review*, 89(5) (2011), 70–80.

97 D. M. Abrashoff, *It's Your Ship: Management Techniques from the Best Damn Ship in the Navy*. New York: Warner Books, 2002, p. 50.

98 Y. Martel, *Life of Pi*. Edinburgh: Canongate, 2016.

99 See https://www.cipd.co.uk/podcasts/creating-sustaining-shared-purpose-organisations.

100 P. B. Warr, Happiness and Mental Health: A Framework of Vitamins in the Environment and Mental Processes in the Person. In J. C. Quick and C. L. Cooper (eds), *Handbook of Stress and Health: A Guide to Research and Practice*. London and New York: Wiley, 2017, pp. 57–74.

101 S. Lara-Bercial and C. J. Mallett, Practices and Developmental Pathways of Serial Winning Coaches. *International Sport Coaching Journal*, 3(3) (2016), 221–239.

102 Deloitte, *The 2017 Deloitte Millennial Survey. Apprehensive Millennials: Seeking Stability and Opportunities in an Uncertain World*. Available at: https://www2.deloitte.com/content/dam/Deloitte/global/Documents/About-Deloitte/gx-deloitte-millennial-survey-2017-executive-summary.pdf.

103 See https://www.ted.com/talks/simon_sinek_how_great_leaders_inspire_action.

104 See https://ed.ted.com/on/PhLkXTSA.

Key 7

105 G. Matthews, The Impact of Commitment, Accountability, and Written Goals on Goal Achievement. Paper presented at the 87th Convention of the Western Psychological Association, Vancouver, BC, Canada, 2007.

106 See https://www.youtube.com/watch?v=ciBRcrOgFJU.

107 W. Isaacson, *Leonardo da Vinci*. London: Simon & Schuster, 2017.

108 C. Northcote Parkinson, *Parkinson's Law: Or the Pursuit of Progress*. London: Penguin, 2002.

109 E. Sober, *Ockam's Razors: A User's Manual*. Cambridge: Cambridge University Press, 2015.

110 M. A. Killingsworth and D. T. Gilbert, A Wandering Mind Is an Unhappy Mind. *Science*, 330(6006) (2010), 932. doi:10.1126/science.1192439.

111 T. Buser and N. Peter, Multitasking. *Experimental Economics*, 15(4) (2012), 641–655.

112 D. Allen, *Getting Things Done: The Art of Stress-Free Productivity*. London: Piatkus, 2015.

113 A. Stellman, *Learning Agile: Understanding Scrum, XP, Lean, and Kanban*. Sebastopol, CA: O'Reilly Media, 2014.

114 A. Gawande, *The Checklist Manifesto: How to Get Things Right*. London: Profile Books, 2010.

Key 8

115 See https://www.youtube.com/watch?v=IQlxLBqgFKc.

116 J. Baer, *Hug Your Haters: How to Embrace Complaints and Keep Your Customers*. New York: Portfolio, 2016.

117 T. Hsieh, *Delivering Happiness: A Path to Profits, Passion, and Purpose*. New York: Business Plus, 2010.

118 M. Watkinson, *The Ten Principles Behind Great Customer Experiences*. London: Financial Times Press, 2012.

119 G. Vaynerchuk, *The Thank You Economy*. New York: Harper Business, 2011.

120 J. Richer, *The Richer Way*. London: Richer Publishing, 2009 [1996].

121 F. Reichheld, *The Ultimate Question: Driving Good Profits and True Growth*. Boston, MA: Harvard Business School Press, 2006.

122 P. Goudge, *Employee Research: How to Increase Employee Involvement through Consultation* (Market Research in Practice Series). London and Philadelphia, PA: Kogan Page, 2006, p. 151.

123 N. Nahai, *Webs of Influence: The Psychology of Online Persuasion*, 2nd edn. Harlow: Pearson, 2017.

124 See http://www.tedxaix.com/talks/employees-first-customers-second-vineet-nayar-tedxaix.

Key 9

125 C. Riener and D. Willingham, The Myth of Learning Styles. *Change: The Magazine of Higher Learning*, 42(5) (2010), 32–35. Available at: https://www.tandfonline.com/toc/vchn20/42/5?nav=tocList; H. Pashler, M. McDaniel, D. Rohrer and R. Bjork, Learning Styles: Concepts and Evidence. *Psychological Science in the Public Interest*, 9(3) (2009), 105–119. Available at: http://dx.doi.org/10.1111/j.1539-6053.2009.01038.x.

126 M. Buckingham and D. O. Clifton, *Now, Discover Your Strengths: How to Develop Your Talents and Those of the People You Manage*. London: Simon & Schuster, 2004.

127 R. Schwarz, The 'Sandwich Approach' Undermines Your Feedback. *Harvard Business Review*, 19 April 2013. Available at: https://hbr.org/2013/04/the-sandwich-approach-undermin.

128 M. Bungay Stanier, *The Coaching Habit: Say Less, Ask More and Change the Way You Lead Forever*. Toronto, ON: Box of Crayons Press, 2016.

129 See https://www.youtube.com/watch?v=BRBR3SOzu6M.

130 C. S. Dweck, *Mindset: Changing the Way You Think to Fulfil Your Potential*. London: Robinson, 2017.

131 J. Kruger and D. Dunning, Unskilled and Unaware of It: How Difficulties in Recognizing One's Own Incompetence Lead to Inflated Self-Assessments. *Journal of Personality and Social Psychology*, 77(6) (1999), 1121–1134.

132 A. Bandura and D. Cervone, Self-Evaluative and Self-Efficacy Mechanisms Governing the Motivational Effects of Goal Systems. *Journal of Personality and Social Psychology*, 45 (1983), 1017–1028.

133 See https://www.ted.com/talks/john_green_the_nerd_s_guide_to_learning_everything_online.

134 K. Kohl, Building a SADEL Organisation: The Framework. *Trainingzone*, 18 December 2018. Available at: https://www.trainingzone.co.uk/develop/business/building-a-sadel-organisation-the-framework?utm_medium=email&utm_campaign=TZMON080118&utm_content=TZMON080118+CID_b48464%20e5631c1054dcac4b56baf7aa02&utm_source=internal_cm&utm_term=Part%202%20of%20a%204-part%20series.

135 PwC, More Companies Planning to Ditch Annual Performance Reviews and Ratings, But Will Employees Benefit? [press release], 29 July 2015. Available at: http://pwc.blogs.com/press_room/2015/07/more-companies-planning-to-ditch-end-of-annual-performance-reviews-and-ratings-but-will-employees-be.html.

136 See https://www.ted.com/talks/rainer_strack_the_surprising_workforce_crisis_of_2030_and_how_to_start_solving_it_now.

Key 10

137 R. Plutchik, The Nature of Emotions: Human Emotions Have Deep Evolutionary Roots, a Fact That May Explain Their Complexity and Provide Tools for Clinical Practice. *American Scientist*, 89(4) (2001), 344–350.

138 S. Baron-Cohen, S. Wheelwright, J. Hill, Y. Raste and I. Plumb, The 'Reading the Mind in the Eyes' Test Revised Version: A Study with Normal Adults, and Adults with Asperger Syndrome or High-Functioning Autism. *Journal of Child Psychology and Psychiatry*, 42(2) (2001), 241–251.

139 See https://www.ted.com/talks/celeste_headlee_10_ways_to_have_a_better_conversation.

140 D. W. Merrill and R. H. Reid, *Personal Styles and Effective Performance: Make Your Style Work for You*. Boca Raton, FL: CRC Press, 1981.

141 M. B. Rosenberg, *Nonviolent Communication: A Language of Compassion*. Del Mar, CA: PuddleDancer Press, 1999.

142 R. Wright, *Why Buddhism is True: The Science and Philosophy of Meditation and Enlightenment*. New York: Simon & Schuster, 2018.

143 D. Goleman, *Emotional Intelligence: Why It Can Matter More Than IQ*. London: Bloomsbury, 1996.

144 K. Ferrazzi and T. Raz, *Never Eat Alone: And Other Secrets to Success, One Relationship at a Time*. London: Portfolio Penguin, 2014.

145 See http://bigthink.com/videos/dan-shapiro-how-to-end-every-argument-even-nasty-political-ones.

146 J. Luft and H. Ingham, The Johari Window, a Graphic Model of Interpersonal Awareness. *Proceedings of the Western Training Laboratory in Group Development*. Los Angeles, CA: UCLA, 1955.

147 R. E. Boyatzis, Commentary on Ackley (2016): Updates on the ESCI as the Behavioural Level of Emotional Intelligence. *Consulting Psychology Journal: Practice and Research*, 68(4) (2016), 287–293.

148 R. H. Thaler and C. R. Sunstein, *Nudge: Improving Decisions About Health, Wealth and Happiness*. London: Penguin, 2009.

149 M. E. P. Seligman, *Learned Optimism: How to Change Your Mind and Your Life*. New York: Vintage, 2011.

Key 11

150 G. Klein, *Streetlights and Shadows: Searching for the Keys to Adaptive Decision Making*. Cambridge, MA: MIT Press, 2011.

151 M. Sinclair, *Handbook of Intuition Research*. Cheltenham: Edward Elgar, 2011.

152 A. Bolte, T. Goschke and J. Kuhl, Emotion and Intuition Effects of Positive and Negative Mood on Implicit Judgments of Semantic Coherence. *Psychological Science*, 14 (2003), 416–421.

153 G. Gigerenzer, *Gut Feelings: The Intelligence of the Unconscious*. New York: Viking, 2008.

154 B. O. Hartman and G. E. Secrist, Situational Awareness Is More Than Exceptional Vision. *Aviation, Space, and Environmental Medicine*, 62 (1991), 1084–1089; quoted in D. I. Radin, Predicting the Unpredictable: 75 Years of Experimental Evidence Quantum Retrocausation: Theory and Experiment. *AIP Conference Proceedings*, 1408 (2011), 204–217 at 211.

155 See https://www.ted.com/talks/graham_shaw_why_people_believe_they_can_t_draw.

156 N. Kazantzakis, *Zorba the Greek*. London: Faber & Faber, 2008 [1946].

157 M. Gladwell, *Blink: The Power of Thinking Without Thinking*. London: Penguin, 2005.

158 See https://ed.ted.com/on/otWe6oXv.

159 B. Jiwa, *Hunch: Turn Your Everyday Insights Into the Next Big Thing*. London: Portfolio Penguin, 2007.

160 E. Sadler-Smith, *The Intuitive Mind: Profiting from the Power of Your Sixth Sense*. Chichester: John Wiley & Sons, 2009.

161 A. Dijksterhuis and Z. van Olden, On the Benefits of Thinking Unconsciously: Unconscious Thought Can Increase Post-Choice Satisfaction. *Journal of Experimental Social Psychology*, 42 (2006), 627–631.

162 *Business Insider UK*, Warren Buffett's Best Investing Advice for Beginners, 6 November 2017. Available at: http://uk.businessinsider.com/warren-buffett-best-investing-advice-for-beginners-2017-11?r=US&IR=T/#1-diversification-isnt-always-a-good-idea-1.

163 G. Klein, *The Power of Intuition: How to Use Your Gut Feelings to Make Better Decisions at Work*. New York: Crown Business, 2009.

Key 12

164 D. Ariely and K. Wertenbroch, Procrastination, Deadlines, and Performance: Self-Control by Precommitment. *Psychological Science*, 13(3) (2002), 219–224.

165 S. Denning, *The Leader's Guide to Radical Management: Reinventing the Workplace for the 21st Century*. San Francisco, CA: Jossey-Bass, 2010.

166 See https://www.youtube.com/watch?v=F9qczwJE-Qg.

167 B. Zeigarnik, On Finished and Unfinished Tasks. In W. D. Ellis (ed.), *A Sourcebook of Gestalt Psychology*. New York: Humanities Press, 1967, pp. 300–314.

168 F. Herzberg, One More Time: How Do You Motivate Employees? *Harvard Business Review*, 46(1) (1968), 53–62.

169 M. A. Adriaanse, G. Oettingen, P. M. Gollwitzer, E. P. Hennes, D. T. D. de Ridder and J. B. F. de Wit, When Planning Is Not Enough: Fighting Unhealthy Snacking Habits by Mental Contrasting with Implementation Intentions (MCII). *European Journal of Social Psychology*, 40(7) (2010), 1277–1293.

170 D. Clark, D. Gill, V. Prowse and M. Rush, Using Goals to Motivate College Students: Theory and Evidence from Field Experiments. NBER Working Paper No. 23638 (2016).

171 T. Avnet and A. Sellier, So What If the Clock Strikes? Scheduling Style, Control, and Well-Being. *Journal of Personality and Social Psychology*, 107(5) (2014), 791–808.

172 J. S. Adams, Toward an Understanding of Inequity. *Journal of Abnormal Psychology*, 67 (1963), 422–436.

173 H. Kappes and G. Oettingen, Positive Fantasies About Idealized Futures Sap Energy. *Journal of Experimental Social Psychology*, 47 (2011), 719–729.

174 Elrod, *The Miracle Morning*.

175 See https://www.tedxtum.com/past-events/tedxtum-2016-entelechy/motivate-yourself-with-visions-goals-and-willpower.

176 C. Foster, In the Wake of Leander: Swimming the Hellespont, 2 February 2011. Available at: http://www.charlesfoster.co.uk/?p=1.

177 D. H. Pink, *Drive: The Surprising Truth About What Motivates Us*. Edinburgh: Canongate, 2011.

178 See https://www.ted.com/talks/dan_pink_on_motivation.

179 T. Sharot, *The Influential Mind: What the Brain Reveals About Our Power to Change Others*. London: Little, Brown, 2018.

180 G. Charness and D. Grieco, Individual Creativity, Ex-Ante Goals and Financial Incentives. Economics Working Paper Series, 2013. Department of Economics, University of California at Santa Barbara.

181 J. Harter and A. Adkins, Employees Want a Lot More from Their Managers, *Gallup Business Journal*, 8 April 2015. Available at: http://news.gallup.com/businessjournal/182321/employees-lot-managers.aspx.

182 D. Ariely, *Payoff: The Hidden Logic That Shapes Our Motivations*. New York: Simon & Schuster, 2016.

183 D. Macleod and C. Brady, *The Extra Mile: How to Engage Your People to Win*. Harlow: Pearson Education, 2007, p. 168.

Key 13

184 T. Bak, The Impact of Bilingualism on Cognitive Ageing and Dementia. In E. Bialystok and M. D. Sullivan (eds), *Growing Old with Two Languages: Effects of Bilingualism on Cognitive Aging*. Amsterdam: John Benjamins, 2017, pp. 243–264.

185 R. Ferguson, Chess in Education: Research Summary. A Review of Key Chess Research Studies for the Borough of Manhattan Community College Chess in Education 'A Wise Move' Conference, 1995.

186 J. Hay, *Working It Out at Work: Understanding Attitudes and Building Relationships*. Hertford: Sherwood Publishing, 2009.

187 J. Gleick, *Genius: The Life and Science of Richard Feynman*. New York: Vintage Books, 1993.

188 J. Dunlosky, K. A. Rawson, E. J. Marsh, M. J. Nathan and D. T. Willingham, Improving Students' Learning with Effective Learning Techniques: Promising Directions from Cognitive and Educational Psychology. *Psychological Science in the Public Interest*, 14 (2013), 4–58.

189 J. Waitzkin, *The Art of Learning: An Inner Journey to Optimal Performance*. New York: Simon & Schuster, 2008.

190 T. Ferriss, *The 4-Hour Work Week: Escape the 9–5, Live Anywhere and Join the New Rich*. London: Vermilion, 2011.

191 See https://www.ted.com/talks/tim_ferriss_smash_fear_learn_anything.

192 See https://www.youtube.com/watch?v=wljRiAofFJ8.

193 See https://www.youtube.com/watch?v=UNP03fDSj1U.

194 D. Coyle, *The Talent Code: Greatness Isn't Born. It's Grown*. London: Arrow, 2010.

195 M. Gilbert, *In Search of Churchill: A Historian's Journey*. London: HarperCollins, 1997, p. 215.

196 S. Adams, *How to Fail at Almost Everything and Still Win Big*. London: Portfolio Penguin, 2013.

Key 14

197 S. Covey, *The 8th Habit: From Effectiveness to Greatness*. New York: Simon & Schuster, 2013, p. 70.

198 Covey, *The 8th Habit*, p. 2.

199 A. L. Tucker and S. J. Singer, The Effectiveness of Management-By-Walking-Around: A Randomized Field Study. *Production and Operations Management*, 24 (2015), 253–271.

200 M. Dodd, *Great Answers to Tough Questions at Work*. Chichester: Capstone, 2016.

201 R. Rosenthal and L. Jacobson, *Pygmalion in the Classroom: Teacher Expectation and Pupils' Intellectual Development*. New York: Holt, Rinehart & Winston, 1968.

202 W. G. Ouchi, *Theory Z*. New York: Avon Books, 1993.

203 R. Tannenbaum and W. Schmidt, How to Choose a Leadership Pattern. *Harvard Business Review*, 36(2) (1958), 95–101.

204 M. Buckingham and C. Coffman, *First, Break All the Rules: What the World's Greatest Managers Do Differently*. London: Simon & Schuster, 2005.

205 K. Scott, *Radical Candor: How to Get What You Want by Saying What You Mean*. London: Pan Macmillan, 2018.

206 C. K. Goman, *The Silent Language of Leaders: How Body Language Can Help – or Hurt – How You Lead*. San Francisco, CA: Jossey-Bass, 2011.

207 See https://www.ted.com/talks/yves_morieux_how_too_many_rules_at_work_keep_you_from_getting_things_done.

208 D. Ogilvy, *Ogilvy on Advertising*. London: Prion Books, 2007, p. 49.

209 J. Womack, *Gemba Walks*. Cambridge, MA: Lean Enterprise Institute, 2011.

210 M. Goldsmith, *What Got You Here Won't Get You There: How Successful People Become Even More Successful*. London: Profile Books, 2008.

211 F. Fabritius and H. W. Hagemann, *The Leading Brain: Powerful Science-Based Strategies for Achieving Peak Performance*. New York: Random House, 2017.

Key 15

212 A. Duke, *Thinking in Bets: Making Smarter Decisions When You Don't Have All the Facts*. London: Portfolio Penguin, 2018.

213 G. Klein, *Streetlights and Shadows: Searching for the Keys to Adaptive Decision Making*. Cambridge, MA: MIT Press, 2011.

214 S. Danziger, J. Levav and L. Avnaim-Pesso, Extraneous Factors in Judicial Decisions. *Proceedings of the National Academy of Sciences of the United States of America*, 108 (2011), 6889–6892.

215 R. Kane, *A Contemporary Introduction to Free Will*. New York: Oxford, 2005, p. 37.

216 G. McKeown, *Essentialism: The Disciplined Pursuit of Less*. London: Virgin Books, 2014.

217 D. G. Ullman, *Making Robust Decisions: Decision Management for Technical, Business, and Service Teams*. Oxford: Trafford Publishing, 2006.

218 R. Buehler, D. Griffin, K. C. H. Lam and J. Deslauriers, Perspectives On Prediction: Does Third-Person Imagery Improve Task Completion Estimates? *Organizational Behavior and Human Decision Processes*, 117 (2012), 138–149.

219 P. W. Holland, Statistics and Causal Inference. *Journal of the American Statistical Association*, 81(396) (1986), 945–960.

220 R. Reber, N. Schwarz and P. Winkielman, Processing Fluency and Aesthetic Pleasure: Is Beauty in the Perceiver's Processing Experience? *Personality and Social Psychology Review*, 8(4) (2004), 364–382.

221 E. de Bono, *Parallel Thinking: From Socratic Thinking to de Bono Thinking*. London: Vermilion, 1994.

222 C. Heath and D. Heath, *Decisive: How to Make Better Decisions*. New York: Random House, 2014.

223 J. Smith, Steve Jobs Always Dressed Exactly the Same. Here's Who Else Does. *Forbes*, 5 October 2012. Available at: https://www.forbes.com/sites/jacquelynsmith/2012/10/05/steve-jobs-always-dressed-exactly-the-same-heres-who-else-does/#2d8c12bf5f53.

224 See https://www.youtube.com/watch?v=542qgGgL1s4.

225 D. H. Pink, *When: The Scientific Secrets of Perfect Timing*. Edinburgh: Canongate, 2018.

226 G. Rowe and G. Wright, The Delphi Technique as a Forecasting Tool: Issues and Analysis. *International Journal of Forecasting*, 15(4) (1999), 353–375.

227 T. E. Nygren and R. J. White, Assessing Individual Differences in Decision Making Styles: Analytical vs. Intuitive. *Proceedings of the Human Factors and Ergonomics Society Annual Meeting*, 46(12) (2002), 953–957.

228 D. Ariely, *Predictably Irrational: The Hidden Forces That Shape Our Decisions*, rev. edn. London: HarperCollins, 2009.

229 See https://www.ted.com/talks/ruth_chang_how_to_make_hard_choices.

230 M. Syed, *Black Box Thinking: Marginal Gains and the Secrets of High Performance*. London: John Murray, 2016.

Key 16

231 K. W. Rizzardi, Defining Professionalism: I Know It When I See it? *Florida Bar Journal*, 79(7) (2005), 38–43 at 43.

232 A. Grant, *Give and Take: Why Helping Others Drives Our Success*. London: Weidenfeld & Nicolson, 2014.

233 E. L. Uhlmann and G. Cohen, 'I Think It, Therefore It's True': Effects of Self-Perceived Objectivity on Hiring Discrimination. *Organizational Behavior and Human Decision Processes*, 104(2) (2007), 207–223.

234 D. E. Beck, T. H. Larsen, S. Solonin, R. Viljoen and T. Johns, *Spiral Dynamics in Action: Humanity's Master Code*. Chichester: John Wiley & Sons, 2018.

235 S. Q. Park, T. Kahnt, A. Dogan, S. Strang, E. Fehr and P. N. Tobler, A Neural Link Between Generosity and Happiness. *Nature Communications*, 8 (2017), 15964. doi:10.1038/ncomms15964.

236 V. Purdie-Vaughns, C. M. Steele, P. G. Davies, R. Ditlmann and J. R. Crosby, Social Identity Contingencies: How Diversity Cues Signal Threat or Safety for African Americans in Mainstream Institutions. *Journal of Personality and Social Psychology*, 94(4) (2008), 615–630.

237 E. E. Smith, *The Power of Meaning: The True Route to Happiness*. London: Rider, 2017.

238 M. Yousafzai, *I Am Malala: The Girl Who Stood Up for Education and Was Shot by the Taliban*. London: Weidenfeld & Nicolson, 2014.

239 P. McCormick, *Sold*. London: Walker Books, 2008.

240 See https://www.ted.com/talks/frans_de_waal_do_animals_have_morals.

241 See https://www.youtube.com/watch?v=dqMj51Ea1K8.

242 Some 88% of polled consumers said they were more likely to buy from a company that supports and engages in activities to improve society: https://www.fsb.org.uk/docs/default-source/fsb-org-uk/policy/assets/better-business-journey.pdf.

243 R. D. Austin and G. P. Pisano, Neurodiversity as a Competitive Advantage. *Harvard Business Review*, 95(3) (2017), 96–103.

244 A. Tjan, *Good People: The Only Leadership Decision That Really Matters*. London: Portfolio Penguin, 2014.

Key 17

245 G. Rubin, *The Four Tendencies: The Indispensable Personality Profiles That Reveal How to Make Your Life Better (and Other People's Lives Better, Too)*. London: Hodder & Stoughton, 2017.

246 C. S. Carver, M. F. Scheier and S. C. Segerstrom, Optimism. *Clinical Psychology Review*, 30(7) (2010), 879–889.

247 See https://www.ted.com/talks/tali_sharot_the_optimism_bias.

248 A. Berg, *The Impossible Just Takes a Little Longer: How to Live Every Day with Purpose and Passion*. London: Piatkus, 2002.

249 R. Holiday, *The Obstacle is the Way: The Ancient Art of Turning Adversity to Advantage*. London: Profile Books, 2015.

250 S. Hansen, *Train Your Mind: Being Focused, Decisive and Effective* (Practical Resilience Series). Auckland: David Bateman, 2006.

251 M. Curtin, Neuroscience Says Listening to This Song Reduces Anxiety by Up to 65 Percent. *Inc.*, 30 May 2017. Available at: https://www.inc.com/melanie-curtin/neuroscience-says-listening-to-this-one-song-reduces-anxiety-by-up-to-65-percent.html.

252 W. Siems, F. J. van Kuijk, R. Maass and R. Brenke, Uric Acid and Glutathione Levels During Short-Term Whole Body Cold Exposure. *Free Radical Biology and Medicine*, 16 (1994), 299–305.

253 W. Mischel, *The Marshmallow Test: Understanding Self-Control and How to Master It*. London: Penguin Random House, 2015.

254 S. Lyubomirsky and M. Della Porta, Boosting Happiness, Buttressing Resilience: Results from Cognitive and Behavioural Interventions. In J. W. Reich, A. J. Zautra and J. Hall (eds), *Handbook of Adult Resilience: Concepts, Methods, and Applications*. New York: Guilford Press, 2008, pp. 450–464.

255 F. Ozbay, D. C. Johnson, E. Dimoulas, C. A. Morgan, D. Charney and S. Southwick, Social Support and Resilience to Stress: From Neurobiology to Clinical Practice. *Psychiatry* (Edgmont), 4(5) (2007), 35–40.

256 J. H. Fowler and N. A. Christakis, Dynamic Spread of Happiness in a Large Social Network: Longitudinal Analysis Over 20 Years in the Framingham Heart Study. *BMJ*, 337(a2338) (2008), 1–9.

257 B. Brown, *Daring Greatly: How the Courage to Be Vulnerable Transforms the Way We Live, Love, Parent, and Lead*. New York: Penguin, 2007.

258 See https://www.ted.com/talks/kelly_mcgonigal_how_to_make_stress_your_friend.

259 M. Williams and D. Penman, *Mindfulness: A Practical Guide to Finding Peace in a Frantic World*. London: Piatkus, 2011.

260 A. Duckworth, *Grit: Why Passion and Resilience are the Secrets to Success*. London: Vermilion, 2017.

261 S. Pressfield, *The War of Art: Break through the Blocks and Win Your Inner Creative Battle*s. New York: Black Irish Entertainment, 2012.

262 See https://www.ted.com/talks/isaac_lidsky_what_reality_are_you_creating_for_yourself.

263 A. Hutchinson, *Endure: Mind, Body and the Curiously Elastic Limits of Human Performance*. New York: HarperCollins, 2018.

264 S. Peters, *The Chimp Paradox: The Mind Management Programme to Help You Achieve Success, Confidence and Happiness*. London: Vermilion, 2012.

265 J. L. Perry, P. J. Clough, L. Crust, K. Earle and A. R. Nicholls, Factorial Validity of the Mental Toughness Questionnaire-48. *Personality and Individual Differences*, 54 (2013), 587–592.

266 J. Collins, *Good to Great: Why Some Companies Make the Leap – and Others Don't*. London: Random House Business, 2001.

267 B. S. Montoya, L. E. Brown, J. W. Coburn and S. M. Zinder, Effect of Warm-up with Different Weighted Bats on Normal Baseball Bat Velocity. *Journal of Strength and Conditioning Research*, 23 (2009), 1566–1569.

268 See https://www.youtube.com/watch?v=36m1o-tM05g.

269 J. Loehr, *The New Toughness Training for Sports: Mental, Emotional, and Physical Conditioning From One of the World's Premier Sports Psychologists*. New York: Penguin Putnam, 1995, p. 5.

270 D. Rock, *Your Brain at Work: Strategies for Overcoming Distraction, Regaining Focus, and Working Smarter All Day Long*. New York: HarperCollins, 2009, p. 114.

271 See https://www.ted.com/talks/daniel_levitin_how_to_stay_calm_when_you_know_you_ll_be_stressed.

Key 18

272 M. Boubekri, I. N. Cheung, K. J. Reid, C. H. Wang and P. C. Zee, Impact of Windows and Daylight Exposure on Overall Health and Sleep Quality of Office Workers: A Case-Control Pilot Study. *Journal of Clinical Sleep Medicine*, 10(6) (2014), 603–611.

273 B. Zeigarnik, On Finished and Unfinished Tasks. In W. D. Ellis (ed.), *A Sourcebook of Gestalt Psychology*. New York: Humanities Press, 1967, pp. 300–314.

274 M. Hyatt, *Your Best Year Ever: A 5-Step Plan for Achieving Your Most Important Goals*. Grand Rapids, MI: Baker Books, 2018.

275 See https://www.ted.com/talks/tim_urban_inside_the_mind_of_a_master_procrastinator.

276 F. Cirillo, *The Pomodoro Technique*. London: Penguin Random House, 2018.

277 D. Coviello, A. Ichino and N. Persico, Don't Spread Yourself Too Thin: The Impact of Task Juggling on Workers' Speed of Job Completion. NBER Working Paper No. 16502 (2010). doi:10.2139/ssrn.1753027.

278 D. Toth, What's New in Fragrances; To Relax or Stay Alert, New Mood-Altering Scents. *New York Times*, 24 September 1989, H1.

279 R. Raanaas, K. Evensen, D. Rich, G. Sjøstrøm and G. Patil, Benefits of Indoor Plants on Attention Capacity in an Office Setting. *Journal of Environmental Psychology*, 31 (2011), 99–105.

280 O. Seppänen, W. J. Fisk and Q. H. Lei, Ventilation and Performance in Office Work. *Indoor Air*, 16(1) (2006), 28–36. doi:10.1111/j.1600-0668.2005.00394.x.

281 See https://www.ted.com/talks/derek_sivers_keep_your_goals_to_yourself.

282 V. M. Gonzalez and G. Mark, 'Constant, Constant Multi-Tasking Craziness': Managing Multiple Working Spheres. *CHI Letters*, 6(1) (2004), 113–120.

283 C. Newport, *Deep Work: Rules for Focused Success in a Distracted World*. London: Piatkus, 2016.

284 See https://www.ted.com/talks/jason_fried_why_work_doesn_t_happen_at_work.

285 J. Collins and M. T. Hansen, *Great by Choice: Uncertainty, Chaos and Luck – Why Some Thrive Despite Them All*. London: Random House Business, 2011, ch. 4.

286 D. L. Cooperrider and D. Whitney, A Positive Revolution in Change. In D. L. Cooperrider, P. Sorenson, D. Whitney and T. Yeager (eds), *Appreciative Inquiry: An Emerging Direction for Organization Development*. Champaign, IL: Stipes, 2001, pp. 9–29.

287 D. McCullough, *The Wright Brothers: The Dramatic Story-Behind-the-Story*. London: Simon & Schuster, 2015.

288 D. Meredith, *How to Be F*cking Awesome*. Gorleston: Rethink Press, 2016.

289 E. Harrell, How 1% Performance Improvements Led to Olympic Gold. *Harvard Business Review*, 30 October 2015. Available at: https://hbr.org/2015/10/how-1-performance-improvements-led-to-olympic-gold.

290 J. Loehr and T. Schwartz, The Making of a Corporate Athlete. *Harvard Business Review*, 79(1) (2001), 120–128. Available at: https://hbr.org/2001/01/the-making-of-a-corporate-athlete.

Key 19

291 K. Robinson with L. Aronica, *The Element: How Finding Your Passion Changes Everything*. London: Penguin, 2009.

292 S. J. Scott, *Novice to Expert: 6 Steps to Learn Anything, Increase Your Knowledge, and Master New Skills*. Cranbury, NJ: Oldtown Publishing, 2017.

293 See https://www.youtube.com/watch?v=5MgBikgcWnY.

294 R. Greene, *Mastery*. London: Profile Books, 2012.

295 A. Ericsson and R. Pool, *Peak: Secrets from the New Science of Expertise*. New York: Houghton Mifflin Harcourt, 2016.

296 M. Gladwell, *Outliers: The Story of Success*. London: Penguin, 2008.

297 F. Johansson, *The Click Moment: Seizing Opportunity in an Unpredictable World*. London: Portfolio Penguin, 2015.

298 K. A. Ericsson, Deliberate Practice and the Acquisition of Expert Performance: An Overview. In H. Jörgensen and A. C. Lehmann (eds), *Does Practice Make Perfect? Current Theory and Research on Instrumental Music Practice*. Oslo: Norges Musikkhogskole, 1997, pp. 9–51.

299 R. B. Zajonc, The Family Dynamics of Intellectual Development. *American Psychologist*, 56 (2001), 490–496. doi:10.1037/0003-066X.56.6-7.490.

300 D. McRaney, *You Are Not So Smart: Why Your Memory Is Mostly Fiction, Why You Have Too Many Friends on Facebook and 46 Other Ways You're Deluding Yourself.* Oxford: Oneworld Publications, 2012.

Key 20

301 See https://www.ted.com/talks/tom_wujec_build_a_tower.
302 D. Miller, The Stages of Group Development: A Retrospective Study of Dynamic Team Processes. *Canadian Journal of Administrative Sciences*, 20(2) (2003), 121–134.
303 T. Peters and N. Austin, *A Passion for Excellence: The Leadership Difference.* New York: Warner, 1985, p. 166.
304 R. Baron, So Right It's Wrong: Groupthink and the Ubiquitous Nature of Polarized Group Decision Making. *Advances in Experimental Social Psychology*, 37 (2005), 219–253.
305 S. G. Rogelberg, J. L. Barnes-Farrell and C. A. Lowe, The Stepladder Technique: An Alternative Structure Facilitating Effective Group Decision Making. *Journal of Applied Psychology*, 77 (1992), 730–737.
306 D. Sibbet and A. Drexler, *Team Performance Principles and Practices.* San Francisco, CA: Grove Consultants International, 1994.
307 A. S. Pentland, The New Science of Building Great Teams. *Harvard Business Review*, 90(4) (2012), 60–69.
308 K. Blanchard and S. Johnson, *The One Minute Manager.* New York: William Morrow, 1982.
309 See https://med.fsu.edu/uploads/files/FacultyDevelopment_LessonsGeese.pdf.
310 See https://www.youtube.com/watch?v=vjSTNv4gyMM.
311 See https://www.ted.com/talks/joe_gebbia_how_airbnb_designs_for_trust.
312 C. Margerison, D. McCann and R. Davies, The Margerison–McCann Team Management Resource: Theory and Applications. *International Journal of Manpower*, 7(2) (1986), 2–32.
313 L. Gratton and T. J. Erickson, Eight Ways to Build Collaborative Teams. *Harvard Business Review*, 85(11) (2007), 100–109.
314 P. Lencioni, *The Five Dysfunctions of a Team: A Leadership Fable.* Hoboken, NJ: John Wiley & Sons, 2002.

Key 21

315 N. Cowan, The Magical Number 4 in Short Term Memory: A Reconsideration of Mental Storage Capacity. *Behavioral Brain Sciences*, 24 (2001), 87–185.
316 D. Sobel, *Longitude: The True Story of a Lone Genius Who Solved the Greatest Scientific Problem of His Time.* London: Harper Perennial, 2005.
317 K. Ishikawa, *Introduction to Quality Control*, tr. J. H. Loftus. Dordrecht: Springer, 2012.
318 R. D. Behn, The PerformanceStat Potential: A Leadership Strategy for Producing Results. *Australian Journal of Public Administration*, 76 (2017), 268–270.
319 C. M. Arrington and G. D. Logan, The Cost of a Voluntary Task Switch. *Psychological Science*, 15(9) (2004), 610–615.
320 D. Levitin, *The Organised Mind: Thinking Straight in the Age of Information Overload.* New York: Penguin, 2011.
321 See https://www.ted.com/talks/jp_rangaswami_information_is_food.
322 K. Eremenko, *Confident Data Skills: Master the Fundamentals of Working with Data and Supercharge Your Career.* London: Kogan Page, 2018.

323 G. Stasser and W. Titus, Pooling of Unshared Information in Group Decision Making: Biased Information Sampling During Discussion. *Journal of Personality and Social Psychology*, 48(6) (1985), 1467–1478.

324 See https://www.ted.com/talks/david_mccandless_the_beauty_of_data_visualization.

325 P. Nuttall, The Passionate Statistician: Florence Nightingale. *Nursing Times*, 79(39) (1983), 25–27.

326 G. A. Gorry, S. Morton and S. Michael, A Framework for Management Information Systems. *Sloan Management Review*, 13 (1971), 21–36.

327 American Management Association, Companies See Need to Build Analytical Skills in Their Organizations: A Study of Analytical Skills in the Workforce, 2014. Available at: http://www.amanet.org/training/articles/companies-see-need-to-build-analytical-skills-in-their-organizations.aspx.

328 American Management Association, Companies See Need to Build Analytical Skills in Their Organizations.

329 T. Tunguz and F. Bien, *Winning with Data: Transform Your Culture, Empower Your People, and Shape the Future.* Hoboken, NJ: John Wiley & Sons, 2017.

330 L. Webber and M. Wallace, *Quality Control for Dummies.* Hoboken, NJ: John Wiley & Sons, 2006, pp. 42–43.

Summary

331 J. Clemmer, Leadership Competency Models: Why Many Fall Short and How to Make Them Flourish. *Clemner Group*, 2014. Available at: https://www.clemmergroup.com/articles/leadership-competency-models-many-failing-make-flourish/.

332 S. T. S. Ghielen, M. van Woerkom and M. C. Meyers, Promoting Positive Outcomes through Strengths Interventions: A Literature Review. *Journal of Positive Psychology* (2017). doi:10.1080/17439760.2017.1365164.

About the Author

Chris Watson is an award-winning specialist in the promotion of adaptive management skills who founded Endor Learn & Develop in 2002 following a successful career in publishing and higher education. He provides fresh, practical ideas to extend performance at work, delivering results through people for every type of organisation – from emerging small- to medium-sized enterprises (SMEs) through to multinational corporations. Drawing on his background in leadership, psychology, education and the human sciences, he has a proven track record in harnessing potential to help organisations flourish. Incurably curious about all aspects of organisational behaviour, his aim is to strengthen relationships in the workplace by sharing straightforward solutions which people can relate to on a personal level.

As an active member of the national learning and development community, Chris writes for the *Business Matters* publication and is a regular blogger at the Knowledge Bank. A chartered member of the Institute of Personnel and Development, he has an honours degree in psychology and a master's in human resource management. As a keynote speaker, facilitator and coach, Chris regularly presents at regional Chartered Management Institute events, business conferences and HR forums. More recently, he has collaborated with a number of institutions to support employability initiatives and has launched an innovative toolkit for young people on the language of work.

Chris lives in sleepy Lincolnshire in the UK with his wife and four children. In his spare time he enjoys watching stand-up comedy, eating spicy tacos and listening to Nick Cave albums (although rarely at the same time). He is always interested in exploring new ideas to extend the performance of people. If you have any great suggestions for developing any of the adaptive skills listed in this book, drop him a line at: hello@endorlearning.com.

Notes

Notes

Notes

Notes

Notes

Notes

Notes

Notes

Endor Learn & Develop

Established in 2002, Endor has a proven track record in extending employee capability and commitment within every type of organisation – from emerging SMEs and not-for-profit organisations through to multinational companies. Our aim is to strengthen relationships in the workplace and beyond by delivering practical ideas which people can relate to on a personal level. As specialists in the development of adaptive skills, we focus on supporting the core set of behaviours and abilities most valued by today's employers and offer actionable approaches which can be applied across a wide range of different jobs and industries to build flexibility and extend employees' performance in role.

What we do

- Training in adaptive work skills
- Management development
- Behaviour-based learning
- Collaborative team working
- Employee engagement
- Facilitation and feedback
- Personal development profiles
- Psychometric testing
- Innovative learning resources

What our clients say

'Endor's approach and professionalism is first class.'

Operations Director, Innovate Logistics

'In tune with the latest ideas and trends.'

Human Resources Manager, Agrial Fresh Produce Ltd

'They have made a real difference to our business.'

Managing Director, Merrick and Day Ltd

'Their emphasis on applied techniques is both engaging and informative.'

Head of Service, York City Council

'Their leadership programme really helped us to understand ourselves.'

Head of Human Resources, Hodgson Sealants Ltd

Creating conversations
and making connections

www.endorlearning.com